Billingsley, Brampton and Beyond

In Search of The Weston Connection

Billingsley, Brampton and Beyond

In Search of The Weston Connection

The provenance of a porcelain service,
over 200 years old, is investigated

Pamela (Theophilus) Gardner

Matador
5 Weir Road
Kibworth Beauchamp
Leicester LE8 0lQ, UK
Tel: (+44) 116 279 2299
Email: books@troubador.co.uk
Web: www.troubador.co.uk/matador

ISBN 978-1848763-470

A Cataloguing-in-Publication (CIP) catalogue record for this book
is available from the British Library.

Typeset in 11.5pt Book Antiqua by Troubador Publishing Ltd, Leicester, UK

Matador is an imprint of Troubador Publishing Ltd

To my husband
David
without whose help and encouragement this book
would not have been started

and to our grandchildren
Jack & Tess
without whose delightful company this book
would have been finished long ago

Contents

List of Illustrations

Unless otherwise stated, all pots featured in this book are within private collections.

Preface

Near the start of my interest in ceramics; at a stage when I bought only factory-marked pieces because they were the more easily identified and researched, I bought a Worcester vase. It was painted with white, raised enamel thistles. The vase was unsigned but after some reading I discovered it was possibly the work of Henry Hundley, whose brother George had also been an artist at Worcester. The date of the vase does not now come to mind, but I remember noting that George had possibly died the year previous. I had looked idly at the decoration and wondered whether Henry might have been thinking of his brother as he painted.

That, I suppose, is when I became as interested in the people producing (or connected with) the pots as in the finished items.

I no longer have the vase. My collection, if it is to be so named, comprises a larger number of books than pots: the number of loved pieces that can be kept is severely limited by the number of safe viewing places available.

This book is something of an indulgence; a way of bringing those distant lives and pots closer that does not necessarily require possession. It is also the only way to bring some organization to the ever-expanding number of boxes of research information, and, subsequently, to dispose of all superfluous notes. That is the theory.

The indulgence extends to my not following the conventions of authorship: the referencing system used in the book is based on Harvard but my methods of research, which utilize modern opportunities, mean that a strict adherence to the formalities of the system is not appropriate in every instance; neither is the alternative numbering system, with its Latin abbreviations ibid. (in the same place) and *op. cit.* (in the work cited), which is more suited to articles than to this book. I trust the 'Sources of Information' will make clear how I have evidenced my research, without distracting unduly from the reading. I hope too that I shall be excused for not writing in the third person; 'the author' does not sit well with me. However, it does not follow that content is more subjective as a result; any assumption or conjecture is clearly stated as such.

Assumptions, conjectures, probabilities and possibilities are kept to an absolute minimum. At the end of some chapters, further information is added. This may be because, although factual, it has not been determined to be relevant; conversely, it may be that the information does no more than corroborate that which has already been established in the main text. In either case, it is there as a potential help to other researchers.

CHAPTER 1

William Billingsley

William Billingsley (1758-1828) aroused much interest, and often devotion, throughout his life. Few who know of him today can fail to be moved by his undoubted skill as a ceramic artist and gilder or by his unfailing passion to produce the most beautiful porcelain possible, no matter the cost.

His life and work have been written about in W.D. John's monograph (John 1968) and frequently as a part of books of broader scope on porcelain of the period. I cannot equal what has gone before in that respect, suffice it here to give a brief outline of what is already established and an indication of where this book is going to stray.

William Billingsley was born in Derby of a ceramic artist of the same name and Mary Billingsley. His relatives included an Uncle Samuel Billingsley, a printer and stationer in London. William, the younger, first began his career at the Derby porcelain factory in 1774. During the time he was there, working as a gilder and an artist – famed for his unique method and style of painting roses – he used his own time to experiment with porcelain production, using a small kiln at his home.

He left Derby circa 1795 and, together with John Coke, set up a porcelain manufactory in Pinxton, Derbyshire.

It was in 1799 that he seemingly gave up the manufacture of porcelain, instead concentrating on its decoration in a studio he established in his residence, which was now in Mansfield,

Nottinghamshire. (On occasions, it has been remarked upon that Billingsley was not particularly able academically, based upon the fact that he was known to have written 'Mansfeild'. But it is wrong to make that assumption: the schoolroom rule 'i before e except after c' was not universally applied at that time; there were families of high standing called Feild and Feilding, and Mansfeild was referred to by that spelling in parliamentary papers).

It is the next period, the time spent on his venture of a porcelain manufactory at Brampton-in-Torksey, in neighbouring Lincolnshire, 1802/3 to 1808, that is of special interest in the writing of this story.

Henry Banks was the first to provide financial backing for the Brampton venture and later, in partnership, William Sharpe, Samuel and James Walker, Benjamin Booth and William Billingsley. Samuel Walker became skilled in the building of kilns and in the development of ground colours, though often he is not fully appreciated for the latter achievement.

The dearth of documentary evidence has made for diverse methods of research and the findings have been all the more unexpected and thrilling.

Before moving on with Billingsley to his next place of work, I return briefly to Mansfield. It is generally accepted that he there painted and gilded white porcelain from various factories including, amongst others, Pinxton, Coalport, the French factory 'de la Courtille' and the W(***) factory, so referred to because of the impressed W(***) marks on some of the pieces. The factory that produced W(***) pieces is not properly identified, though a growing number favour the suggestion of Whitehead, made by Dr Geoffrey Godden. A convincing argument for Whitehead is made in Appendix VI, 'A Problem Group of Porcelains' (Godden 1983). It has to be agreed, however, that without confirming evidence that porcelain was made by Whitehead (better known for its earthenware), we cannot dismiss an alternative theory put forward by Michael Bailey – that W(***) comes from not one but perhaps several factories, the unifying factor being that they were all commissions by the same person/s (the mark being a representation of family arms) and often, though possibly not exclusively, destined to go to Billingsley for decoration (Bailey 2006). Research by Michael Bailey continues on this topic and writings exist both prior to and later than the reference given.

I will return to Brampton-in-Torksey during the course of this book. By circa 1808 Billingsley was employed at the Worcester factory. Initially, he was there given freedom to continue with the development of his formula, but, the fragility of the porcelain during firing made it not commercially viable. Pressure was put on him to make compositional adjustments. This did not go down well.

He fled to Wales, to Nantgarw, in 1813, where, with financial backing from William Weston Young and with the continued help of Samuel Walker, he yet again set about building kilns and producing his porcelain. It should be said that these moves were not without problems, for him and others. Debts and the anger of deserted backers meant Billingsley was obliged at times to use the name Beeley/Bealey/Beely in an attempt to avoid detection. Some might argue he was irresponsible and disloyal. But, whatever the view, his readiness to suffer personal hardships (and cause hardships for his family) clearly demonstrates his passion to be unfettered and uncompromising in his quest to make superb porcelain. This was achieved at Nantgarw, but with losses sometimes reaching 90% per firing (as later written by L.W. Dillwyn to Joseph Marryat, in 1849, cited John 1958; Gray 2003; et al) it is not surprising that they were soon suffering financial hardship.

The following year, William Weston Young persuaded Lewis Weston Dillwyn, proprietor of the Cumbrian factory, Swansea, to allow Billingsley and Walker to transfer production of the porcelain to Swansea. Two new kilns were built on adjoining land for the purpose. Billingsley and Walker stayed at Swansea for three years. However, during that time and almost from the start, alterations to the paste formula were made, evidenced by the products of the factory and supported by the notebooks of Lewis Weston Dillwyn: it appears to have been Dillwyn and Samuel Walker, not William Billingsley, who were in charge of the experimentations.

Given that the Nantgarw body was as close to Billingsley's ideal as he ever achieved, there were, nevertheless, two expedient reasons for change: by producing for Dillwyn a porcelain of the composition experimented on whilst employed by the Worcester factory, Billingsley and Walker had broken the agreement with the Worcester proprietors never to produce this for anyone else (however, they were permitted to produce for themselves). And, of course, there was still an argument for developing a body less likely to lose its shape, or be otherwise damaged, in the kiln.

It is not known to what extent Billingsley was dissatisfied with not being able to produce his beloved Nantgarw type porcelain. But in any case, as a result in a change in responsibilities and commitments for Lewis Weston Dillwyn after the death of his father-in-law, John Llewelyn, in 1817, porcelain manufacture at Swansea came to an end (Gray 2003). In the same year as John Llewelyn's death, Billingsley, closely followed by Samuel Walker, returned to Nantgarw.

Porcelain production resumed at Nantgarw. Much of the successful ware was sold in the white – decorated elsewhere. One purchaser of large quantities was Mortlock, in London; Mortlock was also a purchaser of large quantities of undecorated Coalport porcelain. By circa 1820, it seems the competition was too great for John Rose, proprietor and a founder of a factory in Coalport, Shropshire. He effectively bought out Billingsley and his son-in-law Samuel Walker and closed down Nantgarw.

Sadly, William Billingsley's daughters, Sarah and Lavinia, were now both dead: Sarah, the eldest and wife of Samuel Walker, had not been strong since the torturous journey from Brampton to Worcester, which, according to a letter written to her mother, she had walked "between 50 or 60 Miles". She died January, 1817; Lavinia was taken ill with a violent stomach pain and died within 21 hours of the onset, September 1817.

Samuel Walker's name can be found on subsequent Coalport factory records and, as William Billingsley was at Coalport when he died in1828, it is the general assumption that he too worked at Coalport from circa 1820–1828.

Documentary evidence about Billingsley is again scarce for the Coalport period, but an increase in Billingsley's style of painting at this time suggests he was influential in some way. It is sometimes argued that he could not possibly have had anything to do with the improved porcelain body or the Society of Arts Award of 1820 as there would not have been sufficient time to produce and submit the pieces. (The award was actually given for the development of a lead-free glaze, though the ensuing factory back stamp infers it was for the new porcelain body.) This is true. But the possibility of an earlier collaboration cannot be ruled out. In fact it is highly unlikely that there was not a time of discussions and forming of agreements beforehand. Who knows how far the discussions extended, or even how far back they began!

The relationship between Billingsley and John Rose is an interesting one and worthy of further exploration. My research is not into this area but a few observations on the subject will not be totally out of context.

A visit by Billingsley to 'near Coalport' in 1801 has been reported (Messenger, 1995); the purpose of the visit being to purchase porcelain in the white, for decoration at Mansfield; a reasonable explanation. Did he consider it necessary to visit all the factories from which he purchased porcelain in the white, I wonder. And how many visits would that take? As far as I know this is the only one, near Coalport, recorded , and this because he was seen. It is hard to imagine that William Billingsley, driven to produce porcelain, would now be content solely to decorate. Could he have had things other than his purchases to discuss, at Coalport perhaps? At this time the nearby Caughley factory was in a state of flux, John Rose having taken over Caughley from Thomas Turner in 1799, and a degree of uncertainty still exists as to the goings on during the following few years; a time of opportunities.

One later visit by Billingsley to Coalport is known of (in 1811) "for the purpose of building a new kiln on the new and reverberating principle" (Haslem, 1876). Presumably the kiln was to be the same as Samuel Walker had built at Worcester for the firing of Billingsley's unstable porcelain; an alternative to the usual muffle kiln. The new one resulted in an enhanced vibrancy of the enamel decoration. The visit was, of course, whilst Billingsley was still in the employ of the Worcester factory, always looking towards the next career move. Although it is reported that no agreement could be reached, "shortly afterwards, Mr Rose had one of the new kilns erected".

It is interesting to note, also, the introduction of pattern number 874 at Coalport, illustrated (Godden 1981) on a covered sugar basin described as being of a rare form: the basin has the 1820 'Society of Arts' printed mark, referred to previously. Pattern no. 874 would be in the pattern book dating circa 1811 – 1820 (patterns 643 – 2/170) and, therefore, although its use could continue later than these dates it would not have been used earlier. Coalport's pattern no. 874 strongly resembles (may even be described as the same as) the pattern on the W(***) cup in *figure 1*, dating circa late 1700s to early 1800s. It was common for factories to copy each other's patterns. It was not usual, however, for a leading factory such as Coalport, to introduce a pattern to their factory pattern books some years after being used by a competitor.

Bearing in mind the known use of W(***) pieces by Billingsley; the uncertainties surrounding his activities at this time; the lack of clarity as to precisely what was occurring at Caughley, I think it wise to keep an open mind as to what level of cooperation there might have been between William Billingsley and John Rose.

Further Information

A will of a Samuel Billingsley, stationer, Chancery Lane (but with properties elsewhere, including in Sussex and Kent) was written 6.9.1769 with a codicil dated 18.3.1770: one beneficiary in particular, namely Peter Waldo of Mitcham, Surrey is worth a mention here.

The will of Peter Waldo of Mitcham, Surrey (but again with properties elsewhere, including Kent) was written in 1795, third codicil in 1803, and names Humphrey Sibthorpe, of Canwick, near the city of Lincoln, and his heirs among the beneficiaries.

Figure 1. W(***) cup

Exley (1970) names Rev. Richard Waldo Sibthorpe, born 1792 at the Old Hall, Canwick, near Lincoln as the earliest known collector of Brampton in Torksey ware; some of his collection had come from his mother.

A Peter Waldo and a Thomas Sharpe, of London, were part owners of a ship named 'Kent' – part of the document is dated 1744. (National Archives)

Exley (1970) notes a jug made to commemorate the formation of (William)'Sharpe and Company' and the opening of the china manufactory. William's grandson, Thomas, was third owner of the jug, the fifth was C. L. Exley, when it eventually left the family.

1757 – Samuel Billingsley of the Liberty of the Rolls, stationer, has an interest in the property of Sedge Mead, part of the Maison Dieu (A_2A Lincolnshire archives, Jarvis: The Jarvis papers in these archives cover the period 1321 – 1918 and named places in addition to Lincolnshire include Kent, Warwickshire, Coventry and Yorkshire. Members of the *extended family take the story to numerous other archives in this country and abroad).*

National Archives, Kew, show that Samuel Billingsley, London, stationer was granted Liberty of the Rolls in 1733.

David Manchip has written several articles on the families of the Pinxton area and the related workmen and women of the factory. They are certainly worth a read if they can be located.

CHAPTER 2

The 'Weston Service'

The existence of the 'Weston service', *fig 2*, is, perhaps, still little known: its emergence was a quiet affair.

In the catalogue of 'Tennant's Autumn Sale' of 2005 the lot was described as a French empire part tea/coffee service from the Parisian factory of 'Rue Fontaine – au -Roy' *sic* (this factory is also known by the name 'de la Courtille'). The factory mark of two blue crossed flambeaux, *fig 3*, was on the teapot. However, the French attribution for much of the service was questioned when it was examined by one of Tennant's specialists in ceramics, prior to display for pre-auction viewing. On the day of the auction the auctioneer advised potential buyers to ignore the catalogue description and estimate. An acknowledgment that it was in fact a composite service of both French and English pieces had affected the level of interest and registered bids forced an opening bid of more than double the previous lower estimate. (This was despite no mention being made of the accompanying provenance.)

It is not difficult to explain the level of interest:

- Several decorating establishments of high repute bought French porcelain in the white, William Billingsley included. His use of French porcelain from this particular French factory is well recorded; for example, the complete 'Surgeon Boot' service – decorated in Lincolnshire in the early nineteenth century.

Figure 2. The Weston Service: photograph courtesy of Tennants

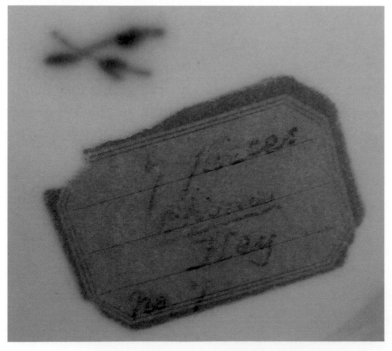

Figure 3. De La Courtille factory mark

- It is also known for services from the Pinxton factory to include pieces made at other factories, Coalport and Spode being two, although the circumstances which led to the presence of such pieces is not always clear; whether wares from other factories were used to supplement Pinxton production at any time, or whether they were simply replacements.

- The 'Weston service' dates to circa the time William Billingsley was at Brampton. There are very few pieces attributed to Brampton and yet the excavations carried out by archaeologist Roy Chapman, his subsequent painstaking reconstructions and the analyses of fire bricks etcetera, indicate a great deal of activity at the site (Chapman, 1995).

Neither is it difficult to see why no attention was drawn to the accompanying provenance, *fig 4*. It appears that the writer of these few words (and recipient of the service at some point) considered the most important information to be the identification of the factory the potter was trying to 'copy'. The vendor was apparently of the same opinion: when approached, via Tennants, for any available information on the history of the service, the vendor kindly responded but with only the reference for the 'Rue Fontaine au Roi' entry in Chaffer's book on porcelain and pottery marks. Whereas, it is the discreet notes surrounding the description of the factory mark that provide the intrigue:

At the top of the page, written in ink, above the factory details

"China given to me by Mrs. Staveley
Bronze & white China"

This line and the factory details appear to be on a piece of paper which has been stuck onto another page.

Written beneath this, also in ink

"Mrs. Staveley said this China was

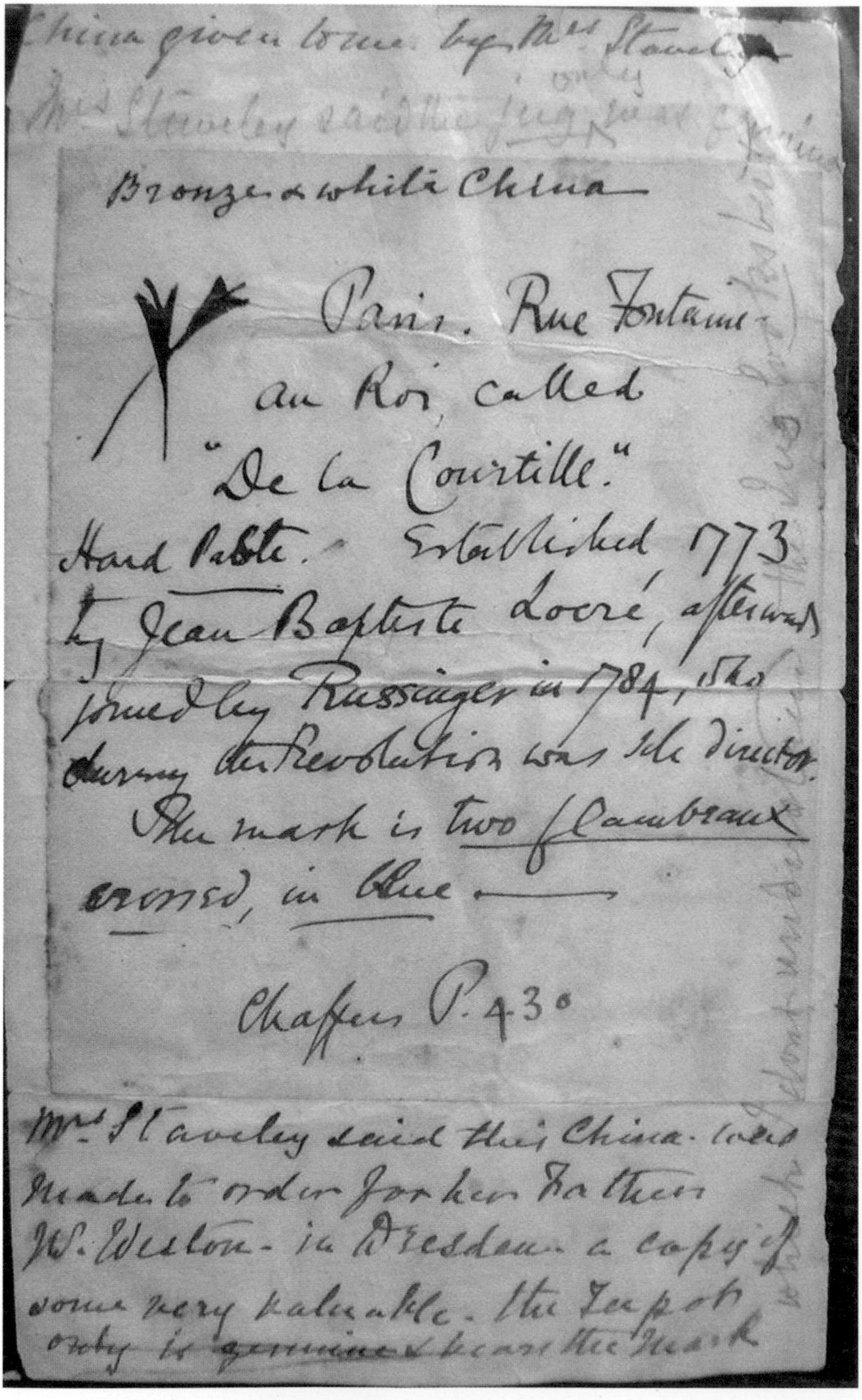

China given to me by Mrs Staveley

Mrs Staveley said this jug was genuine only

Bronze & white China

Paris. Rue Fontaine

au Roi, called

"De la Courtille."

Hard Paste. Established 1773

by Jean Baptiste Locré, afterwards

joined by Russinger in 1784, who

during the Revolution was the director.

The mark is two flambeaux

crossed, in blue.

Chaffers P. 430

Mrs Staveley said this China was

made to order for her father

J.S. Weston - in Dresden a copy of

some very valuable. the Teapot

only is genuine & bears the mark

Figure 4. Provenance

made to order for her father
Mr. Weston in Dresden a copy of
some very valuable the teapot
only is genuine because the mark"

(there is a line through 'only is genuine' but it is not clearly a crossing out)

    Written up the right hand edge, in pencil

"which I dont understand the jug looks best"

    Written across the top of the paper, in pencil (between the two lines in ink)

"Mrs Staveley said the jug only" ('only' is inserted above the line) ?
"just genuine"

N.B. The writer was somewhat confused about the Dresden factories and that of de la Courtille. Their marks were similar – probably intentionally so on the French factory's part – and confusion was quite common at one time.

    Two things are of particular interest; firstly, the name Weston (the gentleman who commissioned the service); secondly, the fact that the request was described as "a copy of", which, presumably, means to be of the same quality porcelain: it is unlikely to refer to the decoration, especially as the jug is described as "looks best"; the jug is arguably the best as regards translucency but not as regards decoration, *figs* 5, 6.

    Although many eminent producers of porcelain experimented with pastes, firings etcetera in order to improve their products, it seems unlikely that they (with the possible exception of Billingsley), would specifically use a French teapot as a template for their porcelain to fulfill an order, which they then included in the final service. More probably, the whole service would be taken from the factory's current production, matching pieces as closely as possible; the decoration being the

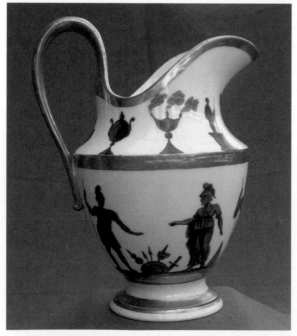

Figures 5, 6. The jug from the Weston Service

characteristic specific to the order. It should be said at this point that the decoration on this service is not unique. I touch on the question of decoration in chapters 8, 13, 14 and the appendix. For the moment, I am suggesting that Mr Weston may have ordered his service from William Billingsley and such a possibility has warranted further research.

Figure 7 shows some of the key people in the life and work of William Billingsley.

William Weston Young and Lewis Weston Dillwyn came on to the scene later than the service. The first recorded contact of William Weston Young with William Billingsley is 1814, when an entry is noted in Young's notebook of money paid to Walker and Bealey (Billingsley). But, as money was changing hands at this stage, an earlier contact between the parties was quite likely.

The relationship between William Weston Young and Lewis Weston Dillwyn is a fascinating one. They had some shared interests (including botany and ceramics) and both mothers were called Sarah Weston – though the dates of the births of William and Lewis and those of their siblings, rule out the possibility of it being one and the same Sarah Weston.

Young leased land from Dillwyn's father-in-law, John Llewelyn, from 1798 until going to work for Dillwyn at Swansea in 1803. The generous and seemingly fluid terms of employment offered to Young were suggestive of a familial relationship but, to my knowledge, none has been recorded. Reference to research on this front is made in the George B. Hammond papers held by the Neath Antiquarian Society.

In some incomplete correspondence dated from February to December, 1936, between George Hammond and Sir Charles Llewelyn, Sir Charles replies that he does not know of any mention of any familial link in letters or diaries, though agrees it looks as though L. Weston Dillwyn and W. Weston Young would be related through Westons. Sir Charles goes on to say that, judging from the notes of Lewis Weston Dillwyn, Lewis believed he came from a line descending from the First Lord Weston (later Earl of Portland). This is explored further in chapter 9.

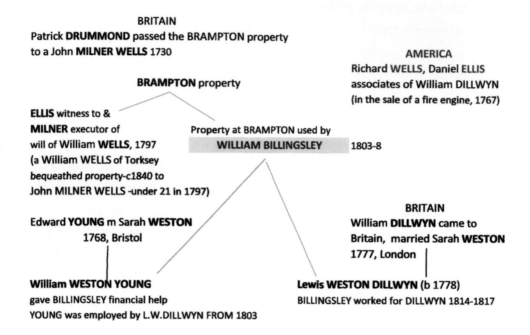

Figure 7. Billingsley links

The porcelain service we will come back to but it is clear, that in order to gain insight into its origins, we need first to gain insight into the people surrounding it.

Further information

Several editions of 'Chaffers Marks and Monograms' include ownership of some specimens. However, none has been found to describe a piece from this service. An Alex Weston is cited in various editions but only in relation to the English porcelains Lowestoft and Lockett (Godden 2008).

CHAPTER 3

Introducing Mrs Staveley

The provenance of the 'Weston service' states "Mrs Staveley gave me this china … … it was made to order for her father Mr Weston". Not a great deal to go on, so, my thanks to Peter Staveley for giving me a start (much of the information on the Staveleys given in this chapter is owed to Peter's research or to pointers it supplied).

There was no record in Peter's research of Staveley genealogy of a marriage to a Weston, but Peter then came up with a page of marriage records which included both the names Weston (Sophia Eleanor) and Staveley (John) – not evidence of their marriage, as the page listed several other names, but a possibility.

A copy of the marriage certificate for Sophia Eleanor Weston confirmed she had indeed married John Staveley, *fig 8*. Her father was William Weston; the groom's father was Luke Staveley, *fig 9*. No other marriage between a male Staveley and a female Weston could be found and all subsequent research has strengthened the case that this Sophia Eleanor Staveley was the Mrs. Staveley who passed on the 'Weston service' to the writer of the provenance.

The exact year of Sophia's date of birth is not known. Census information and a death certificate suggest circa 1802 – 1806. But other information regarding her father, which we come to later, would suggest circa 1800 – 1801 more likely. Sophia was born in Albany, U.S.A, which has been a significant factor in the research.

Not a great deal is known of her life or whereabouts other than a

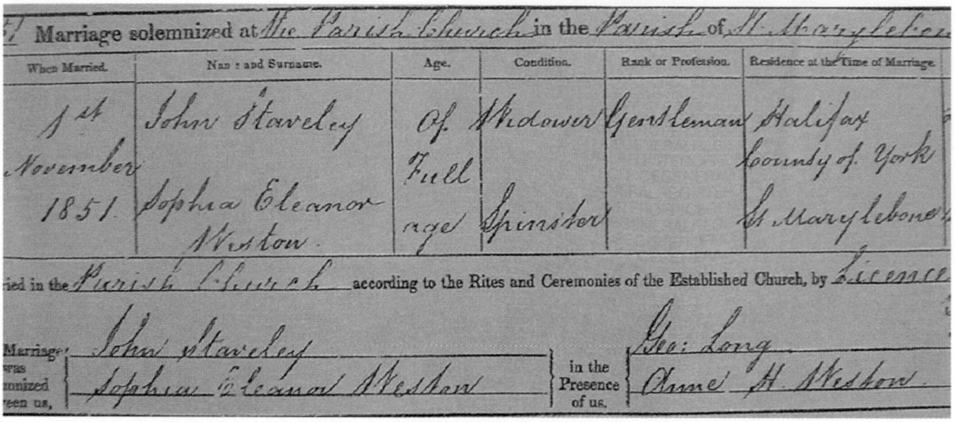

Figure 8. Extract from Sophia Weston's marriage certificate

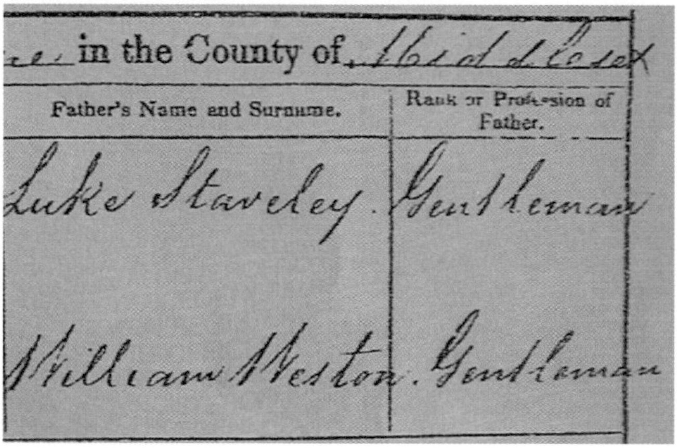

Figure 9. Fathers of the bride and groom on marriage certificate

few dates and names: the census of 1841 tells us that she was living at Nottingham Street, St Marylebone, Middlesex. As the householder with five servants, she was obviously a woman of some wealth. A visitor at the time was a Mary Weston, born circa 1796. Sophia's future husband was, at this time, with his first wife and three children in Halifax.

There was no mention of Sophia in the 1851 census (the census was before the marriage) but John Staveley was now a widower. He was still residing, as the head of household, in Halifax but joined by two sisters from London and a niece.

Sophia E. Staveley, although married, was not residing with John at the time of the census in 1861. She was a visitor at Albion Villas, Folkestone, Kent. Husband John was the head of household at Bleak House, Kings Norton, Worcestershire. The only child still with him was 14 year old John Arthur, a scholar.

John Staveley died in 1870. The 1871 census showed Sophia as a widow staying at the District Grosvenor Hotel in Belgrave. She died in 1872 at St. George, Hanover Square, London.

Mrs Staveley's in-laws

It is pertinent to include some information on Sophia's in-laws, as their circumstances give a flavour of the times in which our protagonists were living and the people with whom they associated.

Sophia's father-in-law, Luke Staveley, 1740-1835, was a political figure as well as a merchant and linen draper: one partnership in this business was North, Staveley & Cotes; another was Staveley & Turner. Luke's political life centered on his support for the rights of the Americans in the American colonies, a particular cause of the Frame makers & Knitters Company of which Luke became a member and liveryman in 1769, and which enabled him to vote in City elections. In 1774 when some two thousand liverymen met at the Guildhall to nominate parliamentary candidates, Luke Staveley urged that they should elect only "known friends to liberty, not by profession but experience". The following year Luke was a main signatory of the Pro-American Petition.

Luke's involvement with the politics of America brought him into contact with such people as William Lee (1739-95), an American Revolutionary Diplomat from Virginia and brother of Arthur, Francis L and Richard H Lee, all revolutionary figures. William Lee and Luke were good friends; William opened a business in London in 1775 and became an alderman as Luke previously had done. Other people Luke may have met, indicated though not fully established, include Benjamin

Franklin; British Commander at Boston, General Thomas Gage; General William Howe and his brother Admiral Richard Howe.

By 1777 the Corporation wanted rid of such radicals as Luke Staveley and he was removed from the Council. However, he remained with the Frame makers & Knitters Company, later moving to Halifax, a key city for the import of Irish yarn.

Richard Staveley (1731-98), an elder brother of Luke's was a druggist, in London, at the time of his death. His premises, on Fenchurch Street, were near to where the East India Company had built a warehouse in 1734. Earlier in his life Richard had, on at least two occasions, held the position of ship's surgeon in the employ of the East India Company (the influence of this company on British porcelain and the interplay with Oriental porcelain is explored in Godden, 1979). He reputedly made quite a fortune in the East Indies, but if this is true he was obviously a man of fluctuating fortunes as he was twice made bankrupt. Throughout his years in London, Richard was regularly visited by Staveleys from Ireland.

(Of purely personal interest is the fact that Richard was one of 150 people to be issued with the first silver racing passes for Doncaster racecourse.)

Another elder brother of Luke's, William (1728-65), went to Jamaica in 1763 and died there in 1765. The same year in which William went to Jamaica, Anthony Staveley there died (Anthony was originally from Ireland). A letter, unearthed by Peter Staveley, offers an explanation for Anthony's death: the letter from the Governor of Jamaica to Whitehall dated April 1763 reports an incident on certain plantations *"whereby rebellious slaves had killed three or four white people"*.

Members of the next generation to also die in Jamaica were two sons of Luke, Richard the younger (died 1804 aged 31) and William the elder (died 1811 aged 46); Luke's nephew Richard Henry Thomas Staveley died in1822 aged 41.

(See chapter 10 and further information after chapters 5 and 9 for other references to Jamaica.)

Sophia's sister-in-law, Anne Staveley (daughter of Luke) married a banker called Henry Hill. The marriage took place in Halifax in 1821. Henry's father, Benjamin Hill was in partnership with the Horderns in the banking company originally known as Hordern and Hill, but which, by 1889 had gone through various changes and had become part of Lloyd's Bank Limited. (Henry's sister, Jane Hickman Hill, married Alexander Hordern at Wolverhampton in 1827. When Alexander died in 1870 he had no surviving children and the family estates passed to Henry Hill.)

It is worth noting here that the families of both William Weston Young and Lewis Weston Dillwyn had interesting connections to large banking concerns, but the context for more details of these is in chapter 9.

CHAPTER 4

William Weston: His Place in History

Who was this man who commissioned the porcelain service? Believed to have been born circa 1763, William Weston was to become a figure of historical significance. His name appears on 'The International Canal Monuments List' prepared under the auspices of 'The International Committee for the Conservation of the Industrial Heritage' (TICCIH) as part of a strategy to identify monuments and sites in categories under-represented on the 'World Heritage List'.

Perhaps typically, more has been written in America about this Englishman than in England. His work there has been widely documented and will be covered first.

In 1792, when Pennsylvanians needed someone to take charge of canal building, they looked to Britain to supply a suitably experienced civil engineer. William Weston was the man they employed, on the recommendation of William Jessop. He sailed from Falmouth to take up a five year engagement as Engineer to the Schuylkill & Susquehanna Navigation Company of Pennsylvania, initially staying at the home of the Honorable Robert Morris; a promoter of the Company, a Member of Congress and Secretary of State. In the event, William Weston stayed in America longer than the five years but did not work solely on the project for which he was first invited.

After only two years the Company became insolvent. William moved to Boston to work on the Middlesex Canal, which ran from

Figure 10. At a Guard Lock

Boston to Lowell. This canal was not completed until 1803 but William Weston did not stay with it the whole of the time. Concurrently, he was involved with the Potomac River Locks at Great Falls (at the personal request of President Washington) and the Western Inland Lock Navigation Company, linking the Hudson River with the Great Lakes in upstate New York. William designed the two intermediate piers for the Schuylkill River Bridge, built by Timothy Palmer. This bridge linked up with America's first major road, the Philadelphia & Lancaster Turnpike; William Weston assisted in the commissioning of this turnpike.

Although William's designs for the particularly deep pier foundations were implemented shortly after his return to England, another of his proposals was not to be acted upon for another forty years. This final plan was a radical scheme to transport water from the Bronx River to New York, terminating in a reservoir in City Hall Park; better able to service the 50,000 residents of New York than the local wells and ponds on which they were still largely dependent.

Reports from America on his work there, suggest that William left America about 1801, not staying to see completion of the several projects with which he was involved. If it was as early as 1801, then Sophia's birth (recorded as in Albany) must have been before the circa

1802 or later, indicated on her death certificate and census returns. Neither his nor Sophia's name has yet been found on a passenger list to confirm when they travelled. In any case, his communication with America on engineering matters was not at an end.

In 1811 William Weston reviewed, by mail, plans for a new canal, the Erie Canal. However, no amount of financial incentive would induce him to accept the offer to be Chief Engineer for the project and this post then fell to Benjamin Wright, the young man whom William had earlier engaged to work for him. Benjamin Wright's success in building the Erie Canal was to earn him the title of 'Father of American Civil Engineering' and it is said that almost all engineers of consequence at that time had trained on the Erie Canal or in New York.

It is fitting then, that America should remember and appreciate William Weston's contributions to American civil engineering history. And significant that, despite some general resentment of the British so soon after the Revolution, very little objective criticism can be found of the man. One supposedly contemporary comment about him has alternatively been quoted as "that haughty Englishman" and "that naughty Englishman". I wonder …

It took longer to discover how William Weston had gained his experience in England. But, any notion I might have had that this 'naughty Englishman' was a mere blagger were dispelled the instant I had sight of his notebook, held at the Institution of Civil Engineers. Examples of pages from the painstakingly constructed notebook are shown in *figures 11 – 14*. It is a general notebook but does include notes on the project that was his main contribution to civil engineering in England: this was as both engineer and architect of the Trent Bridge (as it is now more commonly known. Weston referred to it as the Gainsbro Bridge in his notes; figure 14 is an example page from this work). William's father, Samuel Weston, was engineer for the Oxford Canal and it seems from some reports that William may have assisted him in some way. Also, he may have been instrumental in the building of a turnpike from Gainsborough to Retford. However, the bridge is the only project I have found for which William Weston is the established leading name.

Figures 11 (top) and 12 (below). Pages from William Weston's note book
(Courtesy of the Institution of Civil Engineers)

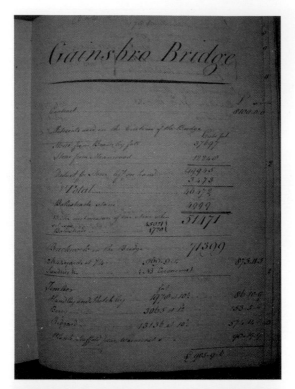

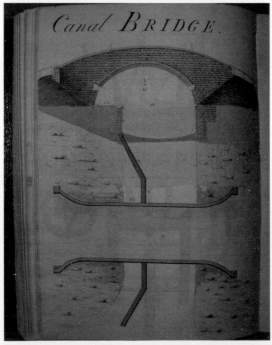

Figures 13 (top) and 14 (below). Pages from William Weston's note book.
(Courtesy of the Institution of Civil Engineers)

A most significant piece of work nevertheless; the Trent Bridge is at Gainsborough, no more than eight miles from Brampton-in-Torksey, the place where William Billingsley was endeavouring to produce his porcelain at the time the 'Weston service' was made.

William Weston produced his plans for the bridge circa 1786: this large three span bridge – its arches spanning 62, 70 and 62 ft. respectively – was built between 1787 and 1791 and is still in use today, *fig 15*. Originally, it was a toll bridge; structurally, it is today much as it was over 200 years ago, except for the addition of a sidewalk (*fig. 16*) in 1964. The bridge now sports a plaque to commemorate this event:

LINDSEY COUNTY COUNCIL
NOTTINGHAMSHIRE COUNTY COUNCIL
GAINSBOROUGH BRIDGE
WIDENED 1964

R.A.KIDD. CBE. B.SC., M.I.C.E. C.K TALLACK. OBE., M.I.C.E.
M.I.M.U.N.E
COUNTY SURVEYOR   COUNTY SURVEYOR
NOTTINGHAM   LINCOLN

On the opposite side of the road is another plaque:

GAINSBOROUGH BRIDGE
ERECTED 1791
PURCHASED OCT. 1927 FOR £130,000
DECLARED FREE FROM TOLLS MARCH 1932
BY P.J.PYBUS ESQ. CBE MP

Yet there is no mention on either of these plaques, or anywhere else on the bridge, of the original architect, William Weston. It's a funny world.

I note here the observation made by Roy Chapman (Chapman, 1995) concerning the site of the Brampton pottery. "In the water-meadow to the west of the site and linking it with the River Trent, there remains clear evidence of a narrow canal of some 100 metres which

Figure 15. (Gainsbro') Trent Bridge today

Figure 16. Sidewalk of Trent Bridge

would have provided safe access to the river; to the nearby port of Gainsborough; and to markets elsewhere for both ware and raw materials" – but I have not yet come across any evidence to suggest that William Weston, canal engineer and architect of the Trent Bridge, was also responsible for that narrow canal.

One of the pages of William Weston's notebook is headed 'Centering – Sawley Bridge' figure 12 – the drawing in figure 13 also appears to relate. There are two Sawleys to have histories of bridges (see also the references to Sawley in chapter 7):

One spans the River Ribble in Lancashire and, like the one in Gainsborough, is a stone, three-arched bridge. It carries a minor road between Sawley and Grindleton and is now Grade II listed.

The other Sawley, with a bridge, is in Nottinghamshire (although sometimes written of as being in Derbyshire), bordering on Leicestershire, near the junction of the River Trent and the River Derwent.

A 'Sawley Bridge' is often referred to today in the latter location (particularly in relation to fishing; for example, 'the weir a little to the south of Sawley Bridge on the Trent' or 'behind the Harrington Arms at Sawley Bridge') but, strangely, contemporary documents relating to a bridge at this Sawley refer to it as the Harrington Bridge. The 'Harrington Bridge' was built in 1790 as a toll bridge. Charges were levied on all except the Earl of Harrington, Lord of the Manor; his servants; and the inhabitants of Sawley and Hemington.

Sawley had been an important village for some time because of its position on the River Trent: The National Archives have a record of a case between Stanhope, Earl of Chesterfield, and De la Fontaine regarding the provision of a landing place on the south bank of the River Trent at Sawley in 1690.

No more is known for certain of the life of William Weston after his letter written in 1811, regarding the Erie Canal, up to his death in 1833, St George, Hanover Square, London.

William's father, Samuel, died in 1804. In his will he requested that he be interred in the family vault at Holwell, Oxfordshire, which promised prospects of useful genealogical information. But a visit to the church there (*fig. 17*) proved disappointing. The churchwarden, Professor Galione, informed me that the church had been rebuilt since Samuel's time and the vault had likely been inside the previous one. In the mid nineteenth century, the congregation had grown too large for the existing church: given the size of the current church (quite small), the original must have been tiny.

Propped up against a perimeter wall in the church grounds was an old headstone, *figure 18*, dated 1850, for the name of Webb. Initially I was glad to see it, as the Webbs were related to a prominent Weston family and took the name of Weston when the Weston line petered out. However, the research at that point also petered out; the wording 'James Webb, the beloved son of Edwin and Ann Webb, died Oct 9 1850, aged 4 years', was a sad reminder of what was typical of the times.

Figure 17. Holwell Church

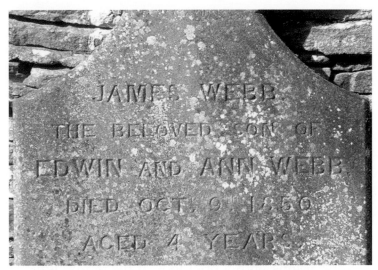

Figure 18. Headstone in the grounds of Holwell Church

Further information

The will of a William Weston of Saint George, Hanover Square, Middlesex, written 1832 and proved 1833, refers to a son Joseph Samuel Weston (his wife Sarah Weston), son William Cowesfield Weston, and daughter Ann Elizabeth Weston.

CHAPTER 5

Notes of Importance

This chapter begins with a brief look at the family which kept safe William Weston's note book from some 200 years ago; the same note book that was discussed in the previous chapter.

A Mrs H.M. Ogilvy donated the book in memory of her brother F.C.S. Montford who was also a civil engineer. The letter offering it to the Institution of Civil Engineers, dated 5th October, 1977, refers to "*the note book written by our ancestor William Weston*". I have identified Mrs H.M. Ogilvy as a grandniece of Samuel Hey, who married Sarah Jane Pratt, the daughter of a Sarah Weston and Rev. Josiah Pratt. As far as I have been able to discover, Sarah Weston is the nearest Weston to Mrs. Ogilvy. The exact relationship of Sarah Weston to William Weston is not known: her father was James Weston of Fenchurch, London at the time he wrote his will in 1822; her mother was Jane Weston, her siblings Jane, James and George. The relevant extract of Mrs Ogilvy's family tree is given in *figure 19*.

Tucked inside a pocket at the front of the note book (along with a letter, which is featured in the next chapter but referred to in the following paragraph) is an undated, unsigned but nevertheless extremely useful note, *fig. 20*. It is written out below:

> *"This charming quaint letter*
> *is from my Great Grandfather*
> *Richard Whitehouse – when*

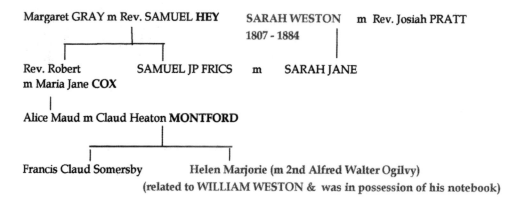

Margaret GRAY m Rev. SAMUEL **HEY**   SARAH WESTON   m Rev. Josiah PRATT
                                                               1807 - 1884

Rev. Robert   SAMUEL JP FRICS   m   SARAH JANE
m Maria Jane COX

Alice Maud m Claud Heaton **MONTFORD**

Francis Claud Somersby   Helen Marjorie (m 2nd Alfred Walter Ogilvy)
                   (related to WILLIAM WESTON & was in possession of his notebook)

Figure 19. Family tree of the keeper of W. Weston's note book

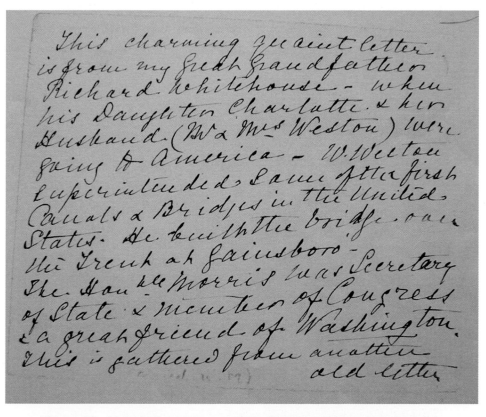

Figure 20. Note tucked into a pocket of William Weston's note book

his Daughter Charlotte & her
Husband (Mr & Mrs Weston) were
going to America – W. Weston
Superintended some of the first
Canals & Bridges in the United
States. He built the bridge over
the Trent at Gainsboro' –
The Honble Morris was Secretary
of State & Minister of Congress
& a great friend of Washington.
This is gathered from another
            old letter."*

The writer of the note is presumably the person who passed on the notebook to the Montfords (Ogilvy), or to their predecessors. Examination of this note, alongside the note which accompanied the 'Weston Service', suggests both notes may have been written by the same person (*figures 21 and 22* are extracts from figure 4):

- The *Mr* shows great similarities and a dash under *Mrs* is present in both notes.
- The *W* of Mr *Weston* differs, but then capital W is written four different ways within the one note of figure 20 (*Whitehouse, Weston, W Weston, Washington*). It is the first W of *W Weston* which resembles the only capital W to occur in the note of figure 21.
- The slight slope forward and the way the capital S is formed, is similar in both notes.
- Capital T is written in two slightly different ways in figure 20 but the way it is written in the *This* at the start of the last line is like the T in *Teapot*, figure 21.
- Similarly, the capital M is written variously within the note of figure 20, but the M in the *Mrs* above the factory mark, figure 22

* *This other 'old letter' would be a good find!*

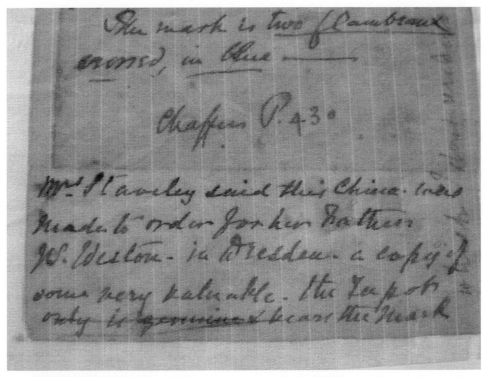

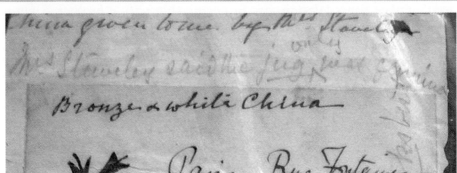

Figures 21 (top) and 22 (below). Extracts from the provenance of
the service

and the M in *Mark* on the last line, figure 21, are similar to the M
of *Mrs* in figure 20.

- The only legible small case g to occur at the start of a word in figure
22 is in the word *given* written on the top line, above the factory
details. It is formed in much the same manner as several small case
gs in the note, figure 20.

It is extremely useful that the writer in this, later discovered, note declares herself/himself to be a great grand-daughter/son of Richard Whitehouse, whose relationship to William Weston we can now deduce.

If we accept the similarity of the hand-writing (we could also include the tendency to write comment without a date or signature), then it can be concluded that this great grand-daughter/son of Richard Whitehouse (Sophia's maternal grandfather) was, at some time, the recipient of both William Weston's service (from 'Mrs Staveley', otherwise Sophia) and his note book.

We cannot assume, however, that the service was eventually passed to the Montford family as was the case with the notebook.

Further information

Sarah's father James Weston was in partnership with a brother Ambrose, attorneys at law. Their premises in 1803 were at Modiford Court, 39 Fenchurch Street, London. A good friend to feature in the wills of both brothers was Richard Sharp of Park Lane, London.

The will of Richard Sharp, with codicils, the latest dated 1835, names a late brother as George Adams Davis; Richard Sharp names Richard Davis as nephew and Marian Elizabeth Davis, niece. Portions of estates in Jamaica; East Indies and some Russian stocks are bequeathed to nephew Richard Davis. (See chapters 3, 9 and 10 for other references to Jamaica.)

James Weston also featured in the will (dated 1833) of George Adams Davis. Richard Davis and his sister Marian Elizabeth Davis are referred to as nephew and niece, respectively, of George Adams Davis.

The name James Weston occurs frequently in Chancery documents, including in a case Weston v Wright, 1808.

CHAPTER 6

In the Broad Vicinity of Brampton-in-Torksey

The precise location of the Pottery House Farm in Brampton is discussed well in earlier works (Exley, 1970; Chapman 1993) but two points are here worth a mention: from the house, if you had faced one direction you would have been looking into Nottinghamshire, faced another direction and you would have seen Lincolnshire. The bridge over the river Trent in Gainsborough (around eight miles from Brampton) is half in Nottinghamshire and half in Lincolnshire, the river being the dividing line.

As has already been pointed out, Trent Bridge is an important association for William Weston to have with Gainsborough. But the bridge is not his only link to the area.

In the will of his father, Samuel Weston, dated 1804 – not long after William's return from America – William is placed in Gainsborough: Samuel describes himself and his younger son, John, as "of Oxford", whereas William is described as "of Gainsborough in the County of Lincoln". This puts William in Gainsborough close to the time when he would have ordered the service.

Samuel leaves legacies to grand-daughters by William; namely Mary, Charlotte and Sophia (I believe the will to refer to three grand-daughters but, as there were no commas written anywhere in the will, I cannot say categorically that it was three not two). William's relationship with Charlotte Whitehouse of Gainsborough may have had something to do with his returning to there.

Lincolnshire archives hold two documents relating to an intended marriage between William and Charlotte; an allegation and a marriage bond: "*William Weston of the Parish of Holywell in the City of Oxford single man aged twenty nine Years … alledged (sic) that he intendeth to marry with Charlotte Whitehouse of the Parish of Gainsborough spinster aged twenty five Years, and that he knoweth of no lawful Let or Impediment, by reason of any Pre-contract, Consanguinity, Affinity, or any other lawful Means whatsoever, but that they may be lawfully married together …*". The bond imposed a financial penalty of two hundred pounds on the groom and his bondsman (Richard Whitehouse) should the allegation prove to be false. These documents, both dated 22nd October 1792, are evidence that a marriage licence was applied for, not proof that it actually took place. However, a later register of marriages does list William Weston's marriage to Charlotte Whitehouse in 1792 at All Saints church, Gainsborough. This would be shortly before he left for America.

He is described (Fitzsimons, 1967) as "arriving in Philadelphia with his bride (perhaps his second wife)". I can find no reason why a first wife should have been supposed, other than a belief, by Fitzsimons, that William would have been almost 40 years old at the time: the information from all American sources that I have come across shows William's date of birth as being around 1753. I have taken it to be circa 1763, as the only primary source that I have of age is the allegation, signed by William Weston in 1792, which gives his age then as twenty nine. The 'Biographical Dictionary of Civil Engineers' also gives his birth at circa 1763. This would, of course, mean that William was a very young man, of only 23, around the time he was responsible for the design of the Trent Bridge at Gainsborough.

The tone of a letter written to him by his father-in-law Richard Whitehouse (merchant and brewer of Gainsborough) suggests a young Charlotte very much under the protection of her new husband. Part of what is a very long letter, is reproduced below:

Gainsbro 3 Dec 1792

Dear Sir

> *Had I the Abilities of a Cicero or Fox, or the best Orator that ever Existed, I could not Express how much I am Obliged to you for your kind and tender care you have taken of My Dear Charlotte previous to Your Embarkation – Your goodness My Dear Sir merits more than every type of Paternal Affection, And I think myself bound under the Strongest Tyes of Gratitude to do everything in my power to add to Your Happiness ...*

...

...

Your Truly Affectionate Hbl. Servant

Richd Whitehouse

It is interesting how little information was needed on the address of the letter, *figure 23*, in order for it to reach its destination.

Figure 23. Addressed to William Weston

The letter from Richard Whitehouse to William Weston was found tucked into a pocket in the front of William Weston's note book, along with the note referred to in the previous chapter.

We now return to the people in the family tree (figure 19) from chapter 5, in particular to Samuel Hey, who became Sarah (Weston) Pratt's son-in-law: there is, at Leeds University, a special collection of letters, most of which were written by Samuel, a renowned surgeon at Leeds Infirmary. (Samuel's uncle, William Hey, preceded Samuel as a doctor of medicine of high repute at Leeds.)

The majority of the letters were written to his elder brother William (who became a Reverend) and are dated from 1828 to 1842. Those in the first batch, dated up to 1831, were from Mr. Cox's school in Gainsborough, which Samuel attended with his younger brother Robert. The maturity shown in one of the earliest letters, 1828, makes it easy to forget that Samuel was only thirteen at the time. A reminder comes when he adds, after discussion on various classical subjects and the books he is searching for on those subjects, that he may have difficulty coming across the books as he is not allowed to leave the playground!

Relations and acquaintances are referred to by the score. However, I have not strained to include them in the following excerpts; any pertinent to the story will, no doubt, surface later.

Notes with the letters, written by a relative, inform us that Samuel calls his father 'The Bishop'; 'The Governor' is his Uncle William, head of the medical practice; plain William is usually his cousin; and 'The Colony' is the vast gathering of relations in Leeds and District.

There are around thirty-four letters, some of which are very long. So, I give below just a few selected snippets, not necessarily the most informative I could find (and not all from Gainsborough) but ones which give some insight into this man who later married into the family of William Weston. Some of the surnames encountered will have become quite familiar by the end of the book:

From Gainsbro' Feb 27 1829

Aunt Rebecca sent me 2 newspapers (some mention of a fire at York Minster). *Joseph Jowett is coming to school here ... 2 of the Metcalfes are day boys ... v. good thing we have got rid of any of them ...*

From Gainsbro' April 29 1829

Mr. Cox has built a coach house and stable. ... (he) *has got a shower bath...Charles Wawn had letter from Mrs. Wawn she says that Mr. Robert Simpson's daughter is dead. ... Mr. James Cox hears us our Euclid ... teaches algebra ... and has our class in Latin ... much more strict than Mr. Cox but I like him very much ...*

From Gainsbro' Jan 22 1831

Mr. Fox going to give Papa pare of black pidgeons (sic)*... From what Papa says of the new house I think you must be rather mistaken about it ...*(I) *went with Papa to see Miss Chappel's paintings ... she is now copying a miniature of Mr. Evans, on a larger scale*

From Gainsbro' July 12 1831

Mr. Fox came ... invited myself and Robert to go to Osmaston ... Papa will come ... go onto Alvaston to take his lecture there ... Richardson Cox was ordained ... saw him in Derby yesterday ... shame can hardly walk.

From Ockbrook (Samuel's home) August 1 1831

Mrs. Wright from America has taken Miss Howton's cottage for 6 months. ... Papa ...has great log of wood ... out of which he has got two rare insects ... and expects to get some more ... I expect to be packed off to York and Kirbymoorside before Leeds ... Robert goes to school on Friday, Margaret on Tuesday in Mr. Roger Cox's carriage with Fanny Cox ...

From Leeds September 26 1831(Samuel went to Leeds Infirmary as a 'dresser' prior to medical school)

... should be mighty sorry to go to school again, especially to Gainsbro' which, upon thoughts of the past, I hate more than ever ... John Hey has been at Ilkley

and is now gone to York, to a meeting of all the Piloso-phosie characters ... in the world. ...Mrs. William and her party came home last week. You need not be afraid of my dying of love for either of Miss Roberts's ...

From Leeds October 29 1831

... The perpetual ticket is 30gns. I have paid 15gns. this year and am to pay the rest next ... I and Croser cannot both go to the same lecture on account of the business ... Papa has bought a horse ... most beautiful action and wants no whip. Sam has also bought a pony in Leeds ... a rum one to the sight, but a good one to go ... (We are) *preparing a famous lot of fireworks for the 5th of Nov, we have made everything ourselves so far ... Had you any rows at Cambridge on account of the rejection of the Reform Bills ... I believe Papa got a good many insects at Halifax tho' I cannot tell you what they were*

From Leeds December 1831

... (I) *still go on playing the organ at St. Paul's ... William had a grand quintelle party ... Colony all well except that Miss Roberts takes ill when she hears anything about the choleras and such bothering for a lot of medicines.*

From Leeds March 8 1832

... I think medical pupils are going to be examined in Greek as well as Latin, chemistry and botany ... Mrs. Simpson is dead ... You asked if I saw much of the female part of the Colony ... I see much of Jane ... not much of others (he remarks, almost illegibly, but certainly sarcastically about 'the adorable Miss Roberts') *... I like Mary Atkinson and Jane very much and I wish the others were like them ... ... Miss Hudson is very well and as fat as ever, she is the greatest glutton I ever saw ... I nearly split my sides with laughing at dinner particularly when Mr.? Jarratt/Jowett was there for he was as bad as her ...*
(Samuel Hey married firstly Martha Jane Jowett, in 1842 and secondly Sarah Jane, in 1868)

From Leeds April 20 1832

... heard from Bob and also Mr. James Cox ... the cholera gets on, I expect it wont be very long before it is at Leeds, there are some cases at Selby, only 20 miles off ...

From Leeds 1833

John Hey will begin his course on Botany ... I shall pay more attention to the subject this year than I did last ... I should collect dry specimens but it would ... take up too much time ... All the Colony pretty well now ... Miss Jane had an abortion about 10 days ago ... you must not mention this in your letter to Ockbrook or to anyone ... John would not be pleased if he knew I had told you

From Leeds 1833

... informing you of the death of ... Sharp of Bradford ... several deaths in and about Leeds ... Old W. Atkinson dead (the father of John Atkinson, solicitor of Leeds) *... Mr. Tennant dying. Macawlay has resigned his seat in Parliament ... appointed to a seat in India. ... Mrs. William has been publishing a book ... title 'The Moral of Flowers' ... I believe* (cost) *about £450 ...If I was William I should be very much vexed but he ...* (is) *pleased with it. Have you heard from the Bishop lately ...*
(This, incidentally, the year of William Weston's death)

From London February 10 1836

... Banker Hudson has set up his cab and tiger and looks as large as life and twice as natural ... he's a good fellow ... I have heard twice lately from Uncle ... about an organ he is having built by Gray, best organ builder in London ... (Gray) *will set off for Halifax ... not quite sure whether he will call at Ockbrook on his way ... he has just been sending a ?layer organ to Philadelphia ... going to build one for some place in Upper Canada ...*

From London August 9 1837

... not knowing exactly where the Bishop is ... send me £10 ... his Lordship to repay you on his return ...our first stage will be from London to Boulogne ... Where does Mr. Evans live in town? All the elections we have anything to do with have terminated horribly ... Little John Hey (going) *to Peckham to commence his school career ... hope happier one than mine ... he certainly will be with a very different Master ...*

From London December 30 1837

... like to visit York better than any place ...Did you see Master Dick? ... your

hint about my waiting to see ...(I was) *always determined to hold my tongue ... might do more harm to say anything ... should not like Richard to know that I ever thought on the subject* (unclear, but it seems Samuel might have been considering proposing to a recently widowed in-law) ... *Mary Jane Jowett had smallpox ... frightened the Pratts ... Till Marianne Pratt's marriage pair going on an architectural tour* ...(Sarah Jane Pratt, daughter of Sarah (Weston) Pratt, becomes Samuel's second wife) ... *May I ask Mr. Evans when he comes to town again for an order to the House of Commons? ...*

From Leeds December 15 1841 (regarding) *Emily ... it is high time she left off the ?- of silver ... blue tinge ... I don't think you would like your wife to attain distinction in this way ...*

From Leeds June 1842
... I did not forget your birthday yesterday ... looking out for particular things ... Grand Square made by Collard and Collard ...33gns ... new ones 50gns ... but was prevented by a female – I was 'Barred' (by Mrs. Barr)! – ... ... I have got the key of my house and have bought sundry articles ... I am doing things v. economically ... bought a set of drawing room rose-wood chairs on sale for £1.14 each ... cost £3.10s each a short time ago ...

The Hey family is of additional interest, not least because of the label on the base of the teapot in the 'Weston service'. The label, (fig. 3), reads

> *7 Pieces*
> <u>*China*</u>
> *Hey.*
> *No 7*

What the wording means is open to interpretation. And Sarah's marriage, of course, post dates the service by around five decades. However, the letters of Samuel Hey were collated and given to Leeds

University Archives by a descendant of Samuel's who helpfully included his own explanatory notes. From these we learn that Sarah Jane was in fact a cousin of Samuel Hey, opening up the possibility of an earlier Weston Hey connection.

There are yet further links with the Westons of the service and Lincolnshire: Sophia Weston's marriage was witnessed by Ann H Weston. This was Ann Henrietta Weston, born circa 1814 (Bath, Somerset), died 1895. At the time of her death she was of independent means living at 107 Gloucester Place, Portman Square, London; an address to also feature in Melbourne and Bulwell estate papers dated 1833, which are held in the Nottinghamshire archives.

In the census of 1881 Ann was head of the household at 107 Gloucester Place (she was described additionally as landowner), with some interesting resident visitors, in particular:

• Mary A. Ingleby.
• Elizabeth Clementson.

Elizabeth Clementson was the widow of John Clementson, both were the parents of Mary Anne (Clementson) Ingleby, by then the widow of Sir William Amcotts Ingilby, 1783-1854, 2nd Bt. of Ripley (the spelling of Ingilby changed in some families around 1870).

The sister of Sir William, Augusta Ingilby, had married, in 1814, Robert Cracroft of Hackthorn, Lincolnshire, the grandson of Charles Fleetwood Weston of Somerby, Lincolnshire. *Figure 24* shows the way in which William Weston is associated with various branches of the Ingleby family and also the Westons of Somerby, Lincolnshire. We return to the Weston family of Somerby Hall in the next chapter.

It does not seem out of place in this chapter to give some more information on the ownership of the property in Brampton–in –Torksey, where William Billingsley was placed at the time the 'Weston service' was produced.

The key family in this regard is the Wells family. The story, as far

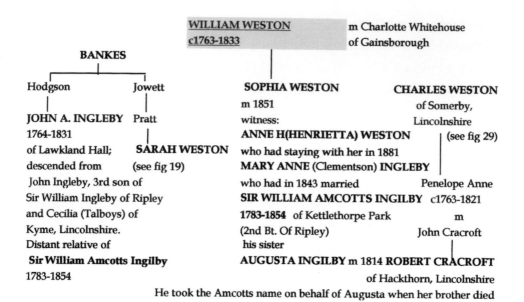

Figure 24. Weston connections to Ingleby/Ingilby

as we know at this stage, begins in 1730 when Brampton Pottery House Farm (though known as Hall Close Farm in 1699 and possibly as such up until 1812) passed from Patrick Drummond to a John Milner Wells and stayed within that family until 1895, when in the possession of Margaret Wells of Lincoln (John W.D. 1968). *Figure 25 is* an expansion of the Wells element of figure 7, chapter 2.

However, the full picture is not quite as simple as this suggests. It is clear from the will of William Wells of Lincoln, dated the 28th October (or December, it is not easily decipherable), 1797, that Mr. Wells is the owner of much property and land: it refers to 'all rents and mortgages' and 'revenue from crops' from 'all my land and estates' but does not specify acreages, or make clear where various terms of tenure (freehold, leasehold or copyhold) may be applied.

It is not surprising, therefore, that other names have been associated with the property and or land: at the time Billingsley moved in, the farm was held by a John Bowmer, though Thomas Nicholson was a tenant of Pottery House Farm in 1805 (Exley C.L.1970). John Bowmer had a life-time lease through his connection to James Ellis,

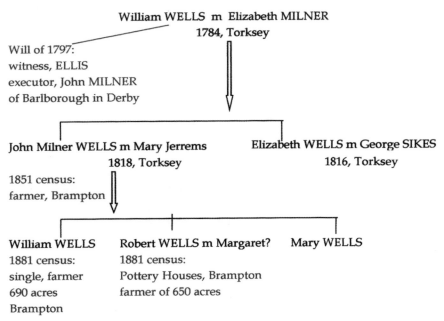

Figure 25. The Wells family of Brampton-in-Torksey

who reportedly owned the farm and was the father-in-law of John Bowmer. Whether we need to probe further into the lives of any of these characters remains to be seen.

The letter of 1811, written by William Weston with regard to the planned construction of the Erie Canal, was directed from Gainsborough. As far as I can discover, there is no later record of his being in this vicinity, and no indication of where he resided up to his death, in London, 1833.

Further information

Two sons of George Ralph Payne Jarvis (the G.R.P. Jarvis of the Jarvis papers referred to previously) namely Edwin, vicar of Hackthorn, and Charles Macquarie, rector of Doddington, married two sisters, Frances Amcotts Cracroft-Amcotts and Augusta Cracroft-Amcotts respectively. The two sisters were descendants of the family of Penelope Anne Weston and John Cracroft (see figure 24).

A brother-in-law of George Ralph Payne Jarvis was Lachlan Macquarie

CHAPTER 7

A Fuller Picture of the Weston Family

What little we know of the members of immediate family of William Weston is largely what has been gleaned from the will of his father Samuel: William had a brother, John, and three daughters, Mary, Charlotte and Sophia. In this chapter, we see what else can be learned.

From the letters of Samuel Hey in the previous chapter, it is apparent that master Hey did not have fond memories of one of the Cox brothers who taught him at his school in Gainsborough.

William Weston's father also seemed to have something against a particular Cox, namely Rebecca Cox. It may be nothing personal, perhaps she was a close relation (note the Cox in figure 19, and also that Sarah Jane and husband, Samuel Hey, were cousins. More Coxes appear later; see figure 51, chapter 9), but, for whatever reasons, Samuel Weston is clear in his will about his wishes.

He bequeaths "*unto my son John Weston of Oxford Esquire all that Messuage or Tenement with the land hereunto belonging situate and being in the Woodhouses in the parish of Frodsham near Chester ... ... other monies ... ... on condition that he shall not nor will intermarry with one Rebecca Cox of the parish of Hollywell in Oxford aforesaid spinster ... ... after the ?decease of my said son then upon Trust to ... ... support the child or children of my said son John Weston lawfully to be begotten on the body of any woman he may happen to intermarry with (except the said Rebecca Cox) ...*" The will was written on the 17th October 1804 and was proved 19th March 1805.

The will of son John was written later that same year (23rd September 1805). His father was dead. John abided by the letter of the condition set in his father's will but certainly not the spirit: "*... my personal estate except my leasehold estate in the parish of Holywell which I hold by lease under Merton College Oxford and my copyhold estate in Woodhouses parish of Frodsham Chester devised to me under my late father's will ... and of my other monies ... and out of the rents and profits of my said leasehold and copyhold estates do and shall pay unto Rebecca Cox who now lives with me ... and every year pay unto the said Rebecca Cox towards the maintenance ... of her daughter Rebecca Weston Cox ...*" A codicil, proved 14th May 1823, along with the original will, provides for a further 4 children: "*... to pay ... Rebecca Cox the five several sums ... towards the maintenance ... of her children namely the said Rebecca Weston Cox Thomas Weston Cox John Weston Cox Mary Weston Cox and Ann Weston Cox ...*". One of the witnesses was a Martha Cox. John does not admit to being the father – they are always 'her' children – but the inclusion of the name Weston; the fact that Rebecca was living with him; plus Samuel's suspicion of John's intentions, leaves little room for doubt. Excepting, there is a certain ambiguity in the codicil of John's will. The main body of the will references his brother William as follows, "*... unto the said Rebecca Weston Cox on her attaining the age of twenty one years but in ?case she shall happen to die under that age then in trust for my Brother William Weston ...*" In the codicil, the wording of the reference to his brother does not make it absolutely clear whether John is referring to a possible legacy for William or to the parentage of Rebecca Weston Cox – "*... the bequests therein contained so far as the same relate to Rebecca Weston Cox daughter of Rebecca Cox and my Brother William Weston therein respectively named ...*".

I interrupt this passage about William Weston's family and the Coxes to remark that, although only a little is told by Jane Austen in her letter to her sister Cassandra (20th November, 1800) of the "*two Miss Coxes*";

too little to enable an identification of them (*"... I traced in one the remains of the vulgar, broad featured girl who danced at Enham eight years ago; – the other is refined into a nice, composed looking girl like Catherine Bigg"*), many other of Jane Austen's acquaintances and family undoubtedly have a rightful place in this book. We meet them in chapter 10.

A return to Samuel but a departure from the Coxes; as noted in chapter 4, in England it was Samuel Weston, rather than his son, William, who was known for work on canals and other waterways.

Samuel was active for over thirty years – until a year or so before his death – and was a respected engineer (working sometimes as surveyor or contractor). Some of the major developments of the times in which he was involved included the Chester, Oxford, Kennet & Avon and London &Western canals. Initially, he worked under James Brindley and he also crossed paths with John Smeaton and William Jessop (as did Christopher Staveley snr, Christopher Staveley jnr and Edward Staveley – these in the areas of Melton Mowbray, Leicester and Oakham. Both Christophers worked in the 1790s. Edward, grandson of the senior Christopher, worked 1825 until 1833, when he fled to America having embezzled funds of the Leicester Navigation Company).

In spite of Samuel's long career and William's relevant obscurity in England the 'Biographical Dictionary of Civil Engineers' surprisingly says of Samuel *'Weston's reputation has tended to be overshadowed by that of his son William'*. The entry under Samuel, 'believed to have come from Cheshire', also makes reference to a Robert Weston, surveyor of Brackley and Aynho, Northamptonshire. The writer was unable to determine the precise nature of their relationship and I have not been any more successful in that respect (but further information is given at the end of the chapter).

Robert Weston and two others bought the lease of the lighthouse on Eddystone. The date of purchase is not known; it may have been quite some time after the death, in 1715, of the previous lessee, Captain

Lovet (see chapter 9 for other Lovetts). However, Robert had some interesting correspondence with John Smeaton from July to September, 1764, largely on the topic of the *"Edystone"* lighthouse:

In a letter from John Smeaton to Robert Weston, John gives a gentle reminder of Robert's *"inclination"* to *"assist Billy Jessop"* and informs him that he (Billy) *"has had no remittances from his Mother for some time"*, which John Smeaton supposes to be because of *"the decrease of trade at Plymouth since the War is over"*. (I have learned from other reading that William Jessop's father, Josias Jessop was employed as draughtsman and modeller for the Stone lighthouse, having previously been involved with the wooden one. He died 1760). Earlier in the same letter J. Smeaton asks R. Weston's assistance in finding employment in a *"Merchants Counting House"* for an unnamed but *"very hopeful young Gentleman"*, the son of J. Smeaton's *"very worthy vicar"*.

Robert Weston's actual response is not amongst the documents but it is clear from J. Smeaton's next letter that Robert had offered more than was expected by way of helping Billy Jessop. He had also helped a Macpherson and a Simon; the latter two are not further identified.

Those providing financial backing for the 'Stone' are referred to by Smeaton as *'Brother Conjurers'*, of whom he names Lord Harcourt, Mr Harcourt and Mr Hoar, alongside Weston of course. The correspondence between them is always warm, and even when Smeaton has exceeded the agreed spend there is no quibble about paying the difference.

The effects of advances in waterways, highways and railways on industries, including the manufacture of pottery and porcelain, are well documented. Those with the vision and the means to invest were often well rewarded. Tolls, such as those levied on the Trent Bridge, Gainsborough, and charges made towards the cost of the lighthouse, seemed a small price to pay for the benefits the users gained.

Letters have been a useful source of information and will be again. But family and estate papers cataloguing, for example, the inheritance, leasing and releasing of properties and land within the often very extensive estates, can be most useful pointers as to which families connect: although it may not always be possible to determine a precise family tree, even if the connection is a familial one.

The family papers of Brooke and of Cholmondeley (Cholmeley), held by the Cheshire and Chester Archives and Local Studies Service, have been particularly useful on several fronts.

The first I pick up on is from a reference, in the Brooke papers, to properties and lands inherited by Samuel Weston but then sometime owned by Sir Foster Cunliffe and T. Brooke, who, by 1812 had surrendered the same to Sir R. Brooke. (N.B. It is apparent that there were at least two Samuel Westons – father and son; William's grandfather and father.)

Sir Foster Cunliffe is a key figure, partly as he enables a connection to be made to the family in the painting of 'The Weston Family', *figure 26*. And as his name will be recurring along the way, it is as well we become more familiar with him at this juncture. The portrait of him, *figure 27*, dates to circa 1787 and was painted by John Hoppner, a celebrated artist of the time.

The internet site of the local government of Wrexham, gives much interesting information on the Cunliffes, some of which is now repeated: Foster Cunliffe, grandfather of Sir Foster and three times Mayor of Liverpool, created a successful family business, trading with the colonies of North America.

By 1720 the company owned four slave trade ships and twelve cargo ships. Foster's son, Robert, took on the role of a director and appointed Richard Morris as manager, under whose management the company continued to flourish. By 1750 they had five trading posts in Virginia and twenty-six ships working the Triangular Trade; their trades included tobacco, Cheshire salt, pig iron, and, unfortunately, slaves from Africa.

The French were willing to buy the poorer quality of tobacco from Virginia that others were not. But they wanted more than the tobacco, they wanted the Cunliffe business. In 1750, Morris was killed as a result

Figure 26. 'The Weston Family' by Benjamin Marshall, 1818

of an accident involving a cannon. It is not quite clear whether or not this was the direct result of one of the frequent skirmishes that took place. In any event, the company went into decline and ceased trading completely in 1759.

It was of little consequence to the fortunes of the Cunliffes. By this time, they had amassed enough wealth to continue living the life of gentry and indulging any philanthropic notions without any great inconvenience.

We now return to the painting of 'The Weston Family', which is held at the Philadelphia Museum of Art. Jennifer Vanim, from the museum, kindly provided results of research on the picture (Dorment 1986).

The painting was exhibited at the Royal Academy in 1819 (no. 241) as 'Portraits of a Family at Little Thurlow, Suffolk' by Benjamin Marshall, 1818. In 1931 Sparrow (cited by Dorment) identified the

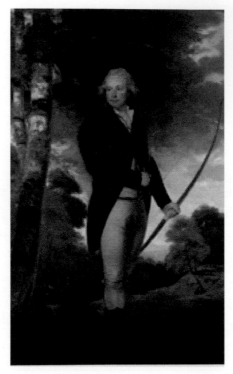

Figure 27. Sir Foster Cunliffe, painted by John Hoppner circa 1787

sitters as the Weston family, presumably repeating information given
by the sellers (Howard Young Galleries, New York, 1930; bt Knoedler
Galleries) to George D. Widener when he purchased the painting in
1930, and the painting is now known as 'The Weston Family'.

A stone slab on the floor of Little Thurlow church is inscribed "IN
MEMORY OF WILL[IAM] WESTON [SON OF] WILLI[AM] [AND
REB]ECCA WEST[ON] WHO D[IED] JUNE 181[?] IN THE [?] [YEAR]
OF HIS AGE." (written as by Dorment). The parish register records the
following burial: "21 June 1817 William Weston of Little Thurlow
buried, aged 23." According to Dorment there is no mention of a
Weston after 1818 in parish records or tithe maps and schedules: neither
is there any mention in *The Gentleman's Magazine* nor any record in the
local will or marriage indexes; which indicates that they were not in
Little Thurlow for very long.

The Westons, therefore, were of sufficient standing to have a family portrait painted and have a commemorative stone slab on the floor of the church, yet they were not the most significant family of Little Thurlow. That honour belonged to the Soames (Soame, Some) family, kinsmen of Soame of Betley and London (Stirnet): Sir Stephen, 1544 – 1619 was one time Lord Mayor of London; his son was Sir William of Little Thurlow. It is at this point, (the introduction of Soames and Little Thurlow), that Sir Foster Cunliffe's connection with Samuel Weston becomes of interest.

There are a lot of marriages from the extended Cunliffe family that connect in some way to our key Weston families. But, for the immediate purpose, I have concentrated on a route (given in *figure 28*) that starts with a member of the Soames family and travels, through Sandys, Fortescue, Throckmorton, Smith, Crewe and Cunliffe to Samuel Weston, William's father.

This establishes a rough connection between 'The Weston Family' in the painting of that name held in Philadelphia and 'William Weston

LITTLE THURLOW: A SOAME, WESTON CONNECTION

		Elizabeth SOAME
		m
Margaret SANDYS	cousin of	William SANDYS
m		
Sir Edmund FORTESCUE		
kinswoman		
Dorothy FORTESCUE (died 1617)		
m		
Robert THROCKMORTON m 2nd		Mary SMITH
Mary's kinswoman & dau of 1st Lord Carrington		Harriet SMITH
		m
E. Emma CREWE cousin of		John Frederick CREWE
m		(1788 - 1840)
Foster CUNLIFFE (1782-1832)		

son of Sir Foster CUNLIFFE, named in the BROOKE family papers, alongside **Samuel WESTON**, father of **William WESTON** of the service

Figure 28. Little Thurlow: A Soame, Weston connection

of Philadelphia' – the manner in which the Brooke family papers refer to him in a transaction of 30 April 1801. However, what that particular relationship is, is not known: at the time of the birth of William Weston (circa 1794), son of William and Rebecca and whose death is written of on the stone slab in Little Thurlow, William Weston, canal engineer and commissioner of the porcelain service, would be married to Charlotte and in America.

It is worth mentioning, that another member of the Soame family, Edmund, married Mary Myddleton (Myddelton, Middleton), great aunt of Richard Myddleton, of Chirk Castle. The provenance of the fine porcelain 'Biddulph Service' circa 1814 -1826 (some pieces of which were sold by Sotheby's, in the London auction rooms, on 5th October 1993) is given by Sotheby's as *"The Biddulph family are recorded in Ledbury and it is possible this service may have been commissioned by the Rev. John Tregenna Biddulph, rector of Mawgan in Cornwall. The family is recorded as having Welsh connections. Sir Thomas Biddulph (1809-1878) was the second son of Robert Biddulph of Ledbury; his mother was Charlotte, the daughter of Richard Myddleton, Esq.,M.P., of Chirk Castle, of the old Welsh family of Myddleton of Gwaynenog."* The 'Biddulph service' is referred to again in chapter 12.

The Fortescue family of figure 28, dates back centuries. Much information on the many, widespread but connected, branches of this family is readily accessible. As happened in many wealthy families, the surname Fortescue is sometimes found to have been adopted, for inheritance purposes, by family members not born with the name. This was usually when the name had been lost on marriage to a family of some standing.

One such instance, of some interest and expanded upon here, is that which stems from the marriage of Dorothy Fortescue (c1699-1733) to Thomas Bury (son of Sir Thomas of Exeter); daughter Catherine Bury married Nathaniel Wells, whose eldest son, Edmund Wells (1752-1779) inherited Fallapit in 1768 from his great aunt Elizabeth Weston Fortescue

(Churchill). At which time he changed his name to Fortescue. (Wells was, of course, the name of the owners of Brampton Pottery House (fig 25) and there are several recorded marriages of Wells with Westons and subsequent names Weston Wells and Wells Weston.) We come across another Fortescue branch of the family in chapter 10 (fig 54).

However, in this chapter we are looking at connections to the known immediate family of William Weston of the porcelain service. In this respect, of more significance is the adoption of the name Fortescue by Richard Inglett in 1777, on inheriting the Spridleston, Buckland and Filleigh estates. Richard had married Elizabeth Weston, whose father, Lucy Weston, was the brother of Edward of Somerby Hall, Lincolnshire, Stephen of Exeter and Captain William (*fig 29*); the significance of Elizabeth's first cousin Charles in placing William Weston, has already been noted (chapter 6, fig 24); and the significance of another first cousin, Rev. Stephen Weston, in relation to the families of William Weston Young and Lewis Weston Dillwyn, will emerge in chapter nine. This is an important strengthening of identified links.

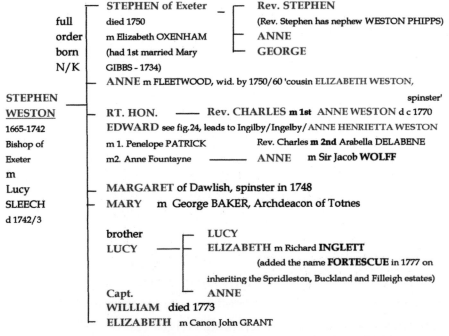

Figure 29. Weston family of Somerby Hall, Lincolnshire

We now return to mentions of Samuel Weston (grandfather) and Samuel Weston (father) in the Cholmondeley family papers:

1729, Samuel Weston of Astmore in Halton, husbandman, is leased property in Woodhouses, Frodsham; for 3 lives; those *"of said Samuel Weston, John Wright, son of John Wright junior of Weston, yeoman, and John Eaton, son of Robert Eaton ... at annual rent of 19/8, 2 rent capons or 2/- and heriot of best beast or good of £3-6-8. Consideration £210 ..."*

1794, Samuel Weston of Oxford, gentleman, is leased for 3 lives properties and lands in Halton ... ... *"were late in the possession of Samuel Weston the elder; for lives of the said Samuel Weston, aged 60, John Weston, son of the lessee, aged 28, and John Wright, son of John Wright of Weston, aged 7, at an annual rent of 9/2 to the Lord of the Manor, and 10/6, one fat hen or 1/- and a heriot of the best beast or good or 10/- to the said Earl of Cholmondeley. Consideration £210 ..."*

The Brooke family papers and those of the Cholmondeley family relate to the same estates and families, at least so far as in the information extracted for this book. I cite one of several documents (A$_2$A Cheshire, Cholmondeley of Cholmondeley) which clearly evidence this; a letter, dated 23 August 1800, from J. Stephens, Agent to Earl Cholmondeley, to Mr Weston, Holywell, Oxford, saying that on the other side (of the paper) is Lord Cholmondeley's Consent to Mr Weston assigning to Mr Brooke the Leasehold Property held under the Earl in Halton and Astmore. ...

Figure 30 includes a fragment of the Wright family tree (Glover 1829): we now see that the mother of Sir Foster Cunliffe was Mary Wright. But of more interest for this section are her nephew John Wright (1758 -1830) of Lenton, Nottingham – son of her brother John – and also the Smith family into which her brother Thomas married. Mary, John and Thomas were all issue of Ichabod Wright (c1700-1777) a banker who owned lands in Nottinghamshire and Lincolnshire. Leonard Jacks,

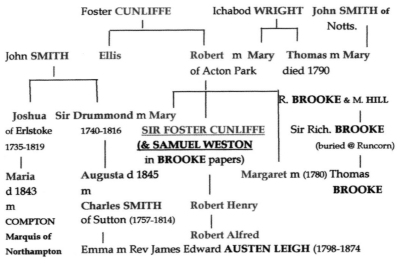

Figure 30. Some important family associations

writing in 1881, believed that Ichabod was engaged in the Baltic trade before founding Wright's Bank, in 1760 (in partnership with his two sons).

Ichabod's grandson, John Wright, kept up the family tradition of banking but in addition, circa 1790/ 1792, founded the Butterley (ironworks and coal-mining) Company, along with William Jessop and two others. A little on the development of the canals around this period is pertinent.

In April 1777 an Act was passed to permit the construction of the Erewash canal from Langley Mill to the river Trent at Long Eaton, which duly went ahead. However, increased industrial traffic through some still difficult stretches of the Trent called for further improvements and in 1783 the Trent Navigation Company was given permission to make such improvements from Sawley up to Gainsborough (the first side cut with locks was finished at Sawley by 1793. See also the references to Sawley in chapter 4). In 1789, parliamentary approval was given for a canal from Cromford to connect up with the Erewash canal at Langley Mill. A link was provided from the Langley Mill on the Erewash with the coal mines of Pinxton and the limestone quarries of Cromford. Nottingham business men preferred to have an alternative route from the Cromford canal, which would go to Nottingham and on into the Trent. So, in 1790 a committee from Nottingham appointed William Jessop, as engineer, to prepare such a route. His first proposal was opposed by Lord Middleton, but by 1792 an Act was passed for the revised Nottingham canal.

It was during the intervening years from the first parliamentary approval and the 1792 Act that John Wright, of Lenton, Nottinghamshire, and William Jessop founded the Butterley Company. Lenton would have been a prime industrial site had Jessop's first proposal been accepted. More on this interesting aspect can be found in the Lenton Times, 1989.

John Smith, the father-in-law of Thomas Wright (son of Ichabod; uncle of John of Lenton) was, like the Wrights, of a banking family. This Smith family also had many, widespread branches and known collateral with our Weston families.

The family connection is of particular relevance when we consider the proprietors and occupants of a residence in Bramcote, a village in Nottinghamshire. A house was sometime tenanted by a Mr Wilmot of the Chaddesden family (Jacks 1881) before he sold it to Frederic Chatfield Smith (of the aforementioned Smith family). Mr Smith built the grand Bramcote Hall on this site, which was occupied by Charles Ichabod Wright (another grandson of Ichabod's) before he moved to Stapleford Hall. The Smith and Wright connection we already know of; Wilmot of Chaddesden is an exciting newcomer.

Chaddesden is a village about two miles from Derby. The Wilmots of this village are related to those of Berkswell Hall, Osmaston, Spondon, Stainsby House and, most importantly, of Trusley (stirnet).

And now, just a few marriages of note, in this context:

1667 – Edward WILMOT of Chaddesden and Spondon married Susanna COKE, daughter of Richard Coke of Trusley.

1718 – Edward WILMOT of Spondon married Catherine Cassandra COKE, daughter of William Coke of Trusley.

Born 1725, died 1759 – George COKE of Kirkby married Elizabeth ELLIS, daughter of Rev. Seth Ellis of BRAMPTON. Of their grandchildren (by son D'Ewes Coke, rector of Pinxton and South Normanton, and his wife Hannah Heywood):

1797 – D'Ewes COKE married Harriet WRIGHT, daughter of Thomas Wright of Mapperley.

1806 – JOHN COKE of Debdale and Trusley, married SUSANNAH WILMOT, daughter of Francis Basildon Wilmot of Trusley and Spondon.

This **JOHN COKE** and the eponymous **BILLINGSLEY** were the founders of the Pinxton porcelain factory, which is referred to in chapter one of this book. (More on the Coke and Billingsley partnership can be found in Exley's book about the factory.)

William Weston and his commissioning of a porcelain service begin to fit into place.

Further information

The will of Robert Weston, dated 1814, gentleman of Aynhoe, Northampton, names a son John Weston. His wife Mary Weston, had a pre-marriage settlement in which it had been agreed she would retain the whole of her own 'fortune'. Robert's 'friends' – appointed trustees and executors of the will – were Samuel Churchill Field and Samuel Churchill, both of the County of Oxford.

The will of a Mary Weston, spinster, Oundle, Northampton, 1818 refers to a late brother Samuel. She also has nephews and nieces named Beale. (Note the William Beale Weston in Chapter 11.)

The will of Samuel Billingsley, stationer (see further information, chapter 1) named Peter Waldo as a beneficiary. In turn, Peter Waldo left legacies to the children of Montague Cholmeley of Easton, Lincolnshire.

Montague Cholmeley (1743 – 1803) of Easton, Lincolnshire married Sarah

Sibthorp, daughter of Humphrey Sibthorp of Canwick (stirnet.com).

Chapter 10 gives further information on the Cholmeleys.

Another beneficiary named in Samuel Billingsley's will is John Russell (the nephew of Samuel Billingsley's wife): one of the witnesses to the codicil is Michael Russell.

*The Dayman family papers, Devon archives, have several references to a John Russell and his brother Michael Russell who have sons John and Michael respectively: Associated with them, in connection with the release of claims on the estate of Reverend John Phillipps, is John **Inglett Fortescue**. (The family documents cover a period back from circa 1200 up to the 20th century but those referred to above are dated circa 1800 to 1840. The probate of a will of a related Joseph Phillipps, 1784, Cornwall Record Office, names other relations which take us into extended families and also back to the Nottinghamshire area. But exploration of those strands is left to another researcher.)*

CHAPTER 8

Benjamin Marshall, other Artists and to whom they may lead

This is not so much a digression, rather it is an opportunity to bring together and comment on, the several artists that are known to link in some way with the people in this story.

I start with **Benjamin Marshall**, the artist of the painting of 'The Weston Family' illustrated and discussed in the previous chapter.

This celebrated artist of horses, and some portraits, was born in 1768, in Leicester. His death was in 1835, the year following the tragic death of his daughter Elizabeth, aged about 22 years: her dress caught fire, from the back, whilst she was looking over her father's shoulder, and she died as a result of severe burns. The shock of this is said to have hastened the death of the artist, who was already widowed; his wife Mary (Saunders) had died in 1827.

Benjamin Marshall left Leicester in 1791 to study under Lemuel Francis Abbott; though it is thought he may have had some earlier training from one of the Boultbee brothers, also of Leicester (Noakes 1978).

John Boultbee (1742 – 1812) and his brother Thomas were both accomplished painters of horses and cattle. Of particular interest to us is John Boultbee's painting of the remarkable and much exhibited animal, the Durham Ox, in commemoration of which many public houses changed their signs. *Figure 31* is an example of Boultbee's picture being used to this day (2008) outside a pub-restaurant in Crayke, North Yorkshire. (Incidentally, this establishment was given the award 'Pub of the Year, 2007/2008'; 2009 is the Chinese Year of the Ox.)

An engraving was made (by J. Wessel) of J. Boultbee's picture and William Billingsley copied it on one side of the important jug made at Brampton, for a Benjamin Wilmot, circa 1806 – 1808. The jug is featured on the cover of Exley's book on Brampton-in-Torksey.

The next artist I come to is the celebrated artist **John Russell** R.A. (1745 – 1806). The Russells were a family of artists and booksellers from Guilford.

One of the ways in which John Russell, probably the most famous

Figure 31. Public House sign of The Durham Ox

of the family, connects to the Westons is shown in *figure 32* – collateral with the descendants of William Weston, one of whom had possession of William's notebook (fig 19). Only one of John Russell's daughters, Jane De Courcey Russell, is featured in that section of the family tree but daughter Anne also married into the same Jowett family. In-law, Dr William Hey of Leeds (first referred to in chapter 6), was a great friend of John Russell's and someone whom Russell visited frequently. It was mostly on a purely social basis but, in 1803, after a bout of cholera had left Russell with some deafness, Dr Hey gave his professional help.

Another Weston and Russell connection is through the marriage of John Russell's granddaughter Hannah to Henry Webb. John Russell, of course, did many portraits and his sitters included several relations. Some sitters of particular note, in the context of this book, are Mary Wood, Arthur Young, James Gurney, Rowland Hill, Sir Richard Hill 2nd Bart. and John Webb Weston. Some of these names we come across again later but Webb Weston is put into context now.

The Webbs first came into the Weston family through Pinchon and Wolffe; a female line from Dorothy Weston when the Earl of Portland title became extinct. (Here we meet with some confusion, which arises

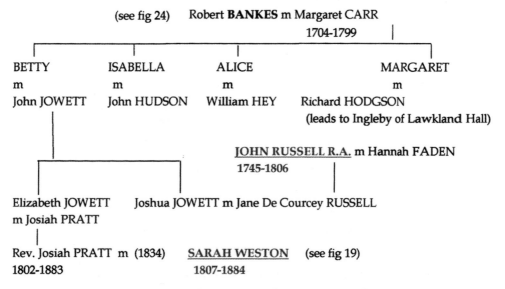

Figure 32. A Weston and Russell connection

because Westons also connected to the next Portland dynasty, see chapter 9). When the Wolffe male line became extinct John Webb added the name of Weston – he was John Webb(e) Weston of Sutton Place, Surrey.

There are several, lengthy, sets of estate and family papers that bring together many of our characters (plus numerous others I have left out for relative simplicity) and which confirm that John Webb Weston is entangled in the web with William Weston of the service. Two key papers are Bradwell Grove Estate papers, Oxfordshire and the Cholmondeley family papers, Cheshire (referred to in the previous chapter in a different circumstance); Pratt, John Webb(e) Weston, Samuel Weston, William Weston, Wells, Hey, Cooper, Brooke, Jones, Hill, Phillips, Sir Edward Coke are but a few of the significant names to occur: the people listed are not necessarily of the places to which the property refers and they are not all of the same status as regards the properties.

I must emphasize that the list of names that connect and interconnect is extensive (and at times cyclical), as are the additional estate and family papers of relevance. There are times when it is necessary to elucidate an association in order to maintain the integrity of the research. However, an attempt has been made to make the salient points whilst keeping to a minimum the tedium of family trees and itemized leases and releases of property. This offer of reassurance is made as I move, indirectly, through John Julius Angerstein, on to the next artists.

John Julius Angerstein is a name that emerged several times during research: some of the instances are given in the notes at the end of this chapter. He was insurance broker; London merchant; connoisseur of art; and philanthropist. And the way in which he connects to William Weston, that is to Sir Foster Cunliffe in the first instance, is illustrated in *figure 33* (note the name Payne and the information at the end of chapter six).

The nuances of this connection will emerge during the course of this chapter.

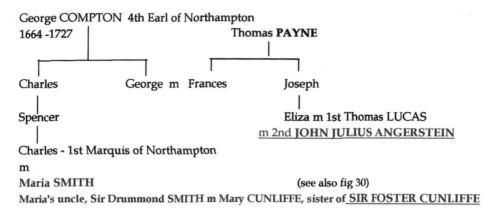

Figure 33. A route from Angerstein to Cunliffe

Angerstein was born, 1735, in St. Petersburg, of much debated parentage: it would serve no purpose here to join in the debate on possibilities. The established facts are that he was brought to London, circa 1749, by Andrew Thomson/ Thompson, a British merchant who was resident in St. Petersburg at the time of Angerstein's birth. Andrew Thomson married a widow Harriet (Buncombe) Wright, who had a young daughter from her earlier marriage, also named Harriet. John Julius Angerstein, the young Harriet and the five children from the Thomson/Wright marriage were as a family unit.

John Julius entered Thomson's Counting House and from that beginning he became one of the underwriters at Lloyd's (1756). Soon prominent at Lloyd's and its chairman for several years, he was later to be known as the 'Father of Lloyd's'; his considerable abilities in marine insurance, coinciding with the time of the wars with France, 1792 – 1815, saw the numbers of subscribers rise from around 180 in 1779 to over 2,000 by the end of the wars. (Policies underwritten by John Julius Angerstein were known as 'Julians'; a clear indication of his contribution and standing.) Angerstein was, at times, both a ship insurer and a ship-owner.

Lloyd's links with Horatio Nelson probably start from when Angerstein headed a management committee for funds to relieve the suffering of the bereaved and wounded after major naval battles, as early as 1794: over £38,000 was raised at Lloyd's following the Battle of the Nile, 1798. Through Nelson, we will come to the artist **Thomas Baxter** (1782 – 1821), but more of that presently.

As a result of the wealth acquired by John Julius Angerstein (or possibly, to some extent, to protect it) he was able to indulge several charitable concerns and subsequently gained the reputation of a philanthropist:

In 1802, John Julius Angerstein, influenced by The Duke of Northumberland's generosity in providing a lifeboat, was responsible for the Lloyd's initiative to give £2,000 towards the installation of further lifeboats all along the coast. The funding of this initiative continued right up to his death (1823). The scheme then (1824) became established as the National Lifeboat Association, under the presidency of the original benefactor, the Duke of Northumberland. As a result of the lifeboats, many lives (and insurance claims) were saved.

Other worthy causes with which Angerstein became involved were taken up equally by some members of his broad circle of influential friends, relatives and acquaintances, which overlapped at points with Weston circles.

The mid 1780s and early 1790s saw the setting up of several committees addressing the plight of black people. These included the Committee for the Abolition of the Slave Trade, later to be known more simply as the Abolition Committee; and the Committee for the Relief of the Black Poor, later known as the Black Poor Committee.

According to information provided by our National Archives, there were up to 20,000 Black and Asian men and women in London by the eighteenth century. Black loyalists who had fought in the American War of Independence were amongst those left destitute after the British defeat in 1782. The antics of such companies as the East India Company, based in London, added to those numbers: sailors working on the ships of such companies were promised their passage home but that promise was not always kept.

Although the Abolition Committee was nominally non-Quaker, it was, in fact, the Quakers on that committee who were the most active. Members included John Lloyd; James and his cousin Richard Phillips (Quaker official printers); Dr Thomas Knowles; Joseph Woods (who married Margaret Hoare); George Harrison (who went to school with Margaret's brother Samuel); importantly, William Dillwyn (father of Lewis Weston Dillwyn) and Samuel Hoare (often referred to as Samuel Hoare Jnr). The latter two members we meet again in chapter 9.

The position and motives of some members of some committees will not be questioned here. But, it has to be noted that one solution – payment to the poor on condition they accepted transportation to Sierra Leone – proffered and acted upon by the second mentioned of these Committees, the Black Poor Committee, proved disastrous for many who accepted the 'offer'.

By mid 1787, both the chairman of the Black Poor Committee, Jonas Hanway, and the proposer of the transportation plan, Henry Smeathman, were dead: Samuel Hoare was now chairman of the committee. John Julius Angerstein was a committee member. Hence, we have a connection between Angerstein and Weston Dillwyn.

At the start of these comments on John Julius Angerstein, his reputation as a connoisseur of art was mentioned. There was a time when his philanthropic interests combined with his association with the Society of Arts: Angerstein (along with others in the 'Superseding Society') was concerned with the plight of the young boys, known as the climbing boys, who were sent up chimneys in order to clean them; a practice that caused the death of, and injury to, many. The Society of Arts, (which had been founded in 1754 for the promotion of arts and also science, in that it could promote productivity and trade), offered a prize for the invention of a machine that could replace their hazardous work. In 1805, one such machine came onto the scene, the Scandiscope. But it was not until after Angerstein's death that the use of climbing boys was eventually outlawed.

In the context of this book, it is Angerstein's patronage of the finer arts that is of more relevance. The interest was shared, and quite possibly influenced by his great friend William Lock.

The Locks were an extremely wealthy family, the consequence of which meant William could enjoy all the privileges of his wealth without the need to trouble himself with industry or trade, unlike John Julius Angerstein. When William Lock's son showed some artistic talent, it was none other than **Henry Fuseli** who offered encouragement to the young William.

Henry Fuseli (1741 -1825) had an eccentric style, maintained throughout his painting career and in his capacities as Keeper and Professor of Painting to the Royal Academy. He had an extensive knowledge of the works of ancient and modern masters, which he conveyed ably to his students. Yet his works were novel creations, described as visionary scenes – that could be playful, romantic and grand; or, grotesque images – capable of creating terror in the mind.

At least two of Henry Fuseli's paintings were bought by Angerstein, circa 1799, (both representations of episodes from Milton's Paradise Lost), though neither was part of the collection bought by the government in 1824, a year after Angerstein's death, which was to form the nucleus of the National Gallery.

In a letter written by Fuseli to William Lock junior, dated 11th August 1800 (Knowles, 1831), Fuseli says *"As it may be expected, and indeed necessary, that I should inspect, and perhaps correct the pictures sent ... to Mr Angerstein's, I take the liberty of applying through you to Mr Lock, to be informed when my admission for that purpose may be attended with the least inconvenience to Mr Angerstein's arrangements ... ... I venture to ask, whether you think it quite impracticable to persuade Mr Angerstein to find a place for 'The Deluge'? It is not quite so wide as the smaller picture in his possession; and though, if placed on the other side of the Satan, it would be less honourable to me than the company of Rubens; it would be more in tune with the rest."*

It is clear from the letter that Fuseli would likely visit the home of John Julius Angerstein at some point. Another visitor to Angerstein's home was Horatio Nelson. The connection between Nelson and Angerstein, through Lloyd's, has already been referred to; a letter, held in the National Maritime Museum, indicates that the connection extended to personal contact. The letter is dated 29th January, 1802 and is written by Nelson, from Merton, Surrey, to John Julius Angerstein in London: *"The first time I come to London I will with pleasure call upon you and as I am sure to be in London before any person is out of bed, I have no fear of not finding you at home, believe me."*

Before we move on from John Julius Angerstein, a reminder of the 'Angerstein service' is pertinent. For readers not familiar with this porcelain, examples of pieces are shown in figures 34 to 38, reproduced with the kind permission of Sotheby's. The plates are of the six lobed-edged shape attributed to the Coalport factory and the figures thought to represent members of the Angerstein family (Godden 1981), though I have no knowledge as to where the service was actually decorated. In addition to both commonplace and fine decoration that took place within the factory, a substantial quantity of undecorated Coalport was sold to outside decorating establishments, including, but not exclusively to those of the Thomas Baxters and Messrs Mortlock in London (see chapter 1). The notion that the figures on this service represent the Angerstein family is supported by the fact that plates featured in figures 34 and 35, when sold in 2003, formed part of the estate of Christopher Rowley of the Rowley family who had married into the family of John Julius Angerstein. The same sale, at Wormington Manor, included three portraits of Angerstein ladies; a portrait of John, son of John Julius Angerstein; a white marble bust of John Julius Angerstein and a painting of horse and stable boy by a painter of the 'circle of John Boultbee'. This takes us back almost full circle to the early part of the chapter.

I promised to return to the artist **Thomas Baxter**. Now is the time. Thomas Baxter enrolled at the Royal Academy as a student in 1800 and did not finish his studies there until 1810. He had work accepted for exhibition as early as 1802, a clear indication of his talent. When his studies were completed, Baxter's book of illustrations of Egyptian, Grecian and Roman Costume was dedicated to his tutor, the aforementioned Henry Fuseli, thus:

Figure 34 (top) and 35 (below). Plates from the 'Angerstein Service'
(Photographs courtesy of Sotheby's)

Figures 36 (top) and 37 (below). Plates from the 'Angerstein Service'
(Photographs courtesy of Sotheby's)

Figure 38. Plates from the 'Angerstein Service'
(Photographs courtesy of Sotheby's)

TO
HENRY FUSELI, ESQ.
PROFESSOR IN PAINTING,
AND
KEEPER OF THE ROYAL ACADEMY,
AS A SMALL
TESTIMONY OF GRATITUDE,
FOR HIS READINESS TO ACCELERATE
THE PROGRESS OF THE STUDENTS
UNDER HIS CARE
THIS WORK
IS RESPECTFULLY DEDICATED,
BY HIS OBLIGED
HUMBLE SERVANT,
THOMAS BAXTER

Goldsmith Street, Gough Square
July, 1810.

Figures 39 to 42 are examples from this book (Baxter 1810).

Figures 39 (top) and 40 (right). Drawings from Thomas Baxter's book on costume, 1810

Figures 41 (top) and 42 (below). Drawings from Thomas Baxter's book on costume, 1810

Baxter is of significant interest to us because of his additional work as a ceramic artist: from 1797 to 1814, Thomas Baxter, alongside his father, also a Thomas, ran a decorating studio in Gough Square, London. It was a highly respected establishment, from which emerged some of the most finely decorated pieces of the time. Ill health was one of the factors which prompted Thomas (the younger) to move to the Worcester (Flight, Barr and Barr) porcelain factory in 1814 (the year following the departure of William Billingsley from there to Nantgarw, discussed in chapter 1). The London studio was closed. A further move was made in 1816, when Thomas Baxter joined William Billingsley at the Swansea factory of Lewis Weston Dillwyn. In 1819, Thomas, once more, returned to live and work in Worcester, until his death in 1821.

To return for a moment to the time when Baxter's work was first exhibited at the Royal Academy, 1802; it was around this time (which, incidentally is also the time of Horatio Nelson's letter to John Julius Angerstein), that Thomas Baxter first received the patronage of Nelson. He was invited to stay at Merton Place, the then home of Nelson and his permanent guests, Sir William and Lady Emma Hamilton. The works that were to come from the sketches and pen and ink drawings he made during that stay include watercolours, enamelled miniatures and splendid decoration on some Coalport ceramics. More on this can be found in the monograph on Thomas Baxter by Wilstead and Morris, 1997; Baxter's sketches from his stay at Merton are held by the National Maritime Museum, with whose kind permission, *figures 43 to 45* are reproduced.

Of less importance, in the context of this book, but, nevertheless, worth a mention, is Philip Ballard, born in Worcestshire and articled to the London decorator John Bradley. He is the likely artist of the 'Biddulph service' referred to in the preceding chapter and again in chapter 12 (R. S.Edmundson, in Gray, 2003).

Further information

Nelson is amongst the list of sitters of John Hoppner, painter of 'Sir Foster Cunliffe' as he is of Benjamin Marshall, painter of 'The Weston Family'. A William Weston, John Julius Angerstein and Robert Heathcote, appear together in Chancery, the documents of which span several years:

Figures 43 (top) and 44 (below). From Thomas Baxter's Merton Place sketch
book
(Photographs courtesy of the British Maritime Museum)

Figures 45. From Thomas Baxter's Merton Place sketch book
(Photographs courtesy of the British Maritime Museum)

Learmouth v **Angerstein**. Ref.C13/105/7 dated 1809
Plaintiffs: Alexander Learmouth and another.
Defendants: William Lock, John Julius Angerstein, Henry Crockett, Anna
Peterella Hartsink, John Reeves, Robert Tabrum, Robert Heathcote,
William Weston, John Wighton, John Paton, John Casper Hartsink
(abroad).
Learmouth v **Heathcote**. Ref. C13/130/44 dated 1811
Plaintiffs and Defendants, as previously listed.
Learmouth v **Weston**. Ref. C13/265/42 dated 1821
Plaintiffs and Defendants, as previously listed.

These extensive documents have not been studied in full but the gist of the
later one seems to relate to the timing of particular bankruptcies and the
apportioning of subsequent liabilities.
A William Weston of County of Lincoln was appointed 'Master Extraordinary
of Our Court of Chancery' in 1825. One of the signatures verifying the
appointment was Robert Michael Baxter.

Angerstein was connected to the Boucheretts through his first marriage. Emilia Boucherett was a close friend of Mary Cholmondeley, who was tragically killed when the carriage in which she was travelling overturned.

CHAPTER 9

Enlightened Networks

William Weston and many other characters to feature in our story were born in the Age of Enlightenment: an age, following on from the Age of Reason, in which improvements in the lives of all were thought possible through education and reasoning; when previously accepted dogma was rejected. Immanuel Kant challenged people to 'Dare to Know'; to examine and question received ideas and values. One could argue that these would be just the sort of people who would want to patronize those artists and potters who were instructive in their work and pushing the boundaries of science. One could also argue that William Billingsley would have been just such a person to attract their patronage.

I have, in previous chapters, touched on the relevance of the people with whom William Weston and his family would have mixed. It is now time to further explore this area. It is no easy task and difficult to find the most suitable starting point, as the paths of so many eminent people converged and diverged across continents, through families, shared professions and shared beliefs.

I think it useful to first look at the families and connections of the other 'Westons' (Lewis Weston Dillwyn; William Weston Young) whose names are so closely linked to that of William Billingsley.

Although a connection through the Weston name has always been thought the most likely (especially as the Sarah Weston who married William Dillwyn was his cousin) it has also been the most elusive. The first connection I found was through the Smith family: the first Richard Smith on *figure 46,* born 1626, was of Bramham, Yorkshire, England but some members of his family, travelled/ emigrated to America, as did members of the connected families.

It is of some interest that Richard's son Samuel (born 1672) married Elizabeth Lovett in the county of Buckinghamshire, Pennsylvania: the family papers of Lovett, Buckinghamshire, England, name Joseph Weston Young of Neath (great-nephew of William Weston Young) as a party involved in the conveyance of property in Middlesex (1862). In an earlier conveyance of property in Middlesex (in 1857) the parties named include Charles Heaton Ellis and, more importantly, William Henry Cavendish, Duke of Portland, deceased.

This, to some extent, supports Lewis Weston Dillwyn's belief that his family descended from the Earl of Portland. But the position is still confusing: the first Portland title went to a Weston but the line became extinct in 1688. When it was revived the following year a Bentinck was made 1st Earl of Portland; the 2nd Earl became 1st Duke and the Cavendishes came into the family by a marriage to the 3rd Duke.

Figure 46 is, of course a diminutive section of the family tree: Richard of Bramham, for example, had at least twelve children. You will note W.W. Young and L.W. Dillwyn is not strictly a blood connection in this figure, as Lewis Weston Dillwyn was an issue from

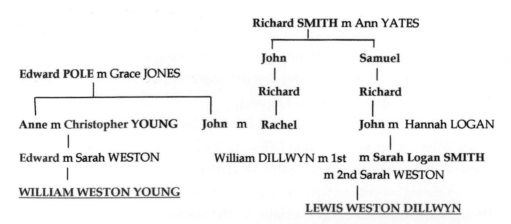

Figure 46. William Weston Young and Lewis Weston Dillwyn connect

William Dillwyn's second marriage, his first marriage was to the Smith; William Weston Young's maternal great uncle, John Pole, married into the same Smith family. This really is of academic interest only. What is apparent is the opportunity for becoming acquainted.

It was William Dillwyn (1743-1824), who in 1802 bought, for his son Lewis Weston, the Cambrian pottery where, some years later, Swansea porcelain was to be produced.

He was born in Philadelphia but moved to Burlington in 1764 when he married Sarah Logan Smith.

William Dillwyn was a Quaker merchant, and like many Quakers, he opposed slavery. His name appears in the papers of correspondence with Benjamin Franklin, a fellow Quaker and opponent of slavery. The year before a visit to London in 1774, Dillwyn wrote of 'the considerations on Slavery, and the Expediency of Its Abolition'. When he next came to England it was to stay: he married his second wife, Sarah Weston, also a Quaker, at the Tottenham Meeting House. (It is a little puzzling that this was allowed if reports are true that Sarah was William's cousin; Friends were often excluded from the Society if they married a cousin. So, presumably, the relationship was distant.) In England, William Dillwyn served as the London agent for the Philadelphia Library Company and continued to campaign for the abolition of the slave trade; he was one of the founders of an anti-slavery committee in London in 1787. (Some others with whom he connected in this work were mentioned in the previous chapter.)

Tottenham Friends were typical of groups of Quakers generally. They included amongst their number highly educated people, working hard and steadfastly to progress, whether it was in business (many household names, such as Barclay, Lloyd, Cadbury, Fry and Rowntree were Quaker families), science or education.

Luke Howard (1772-1864) attended the Tottenham Meetings at times and whether or not those times ever coincided with William Dillwyn's attendance, the two men were surely acquainted with each other: for, in 1796, Luke married Maria Bella Eliot, the daughter of John Eliot and Mary Weston, cousin of Sarah (Weston) Dillwyn.

Luke Howard epitomized the versatility of a high intellect. He is remembered today mostly as 'The Man who named the Clouds'. His 'Essay on the Modification of Clouds' – in which clouds cirrus, cumulus, stratus and nimbus were first so classified – was published in 1803; he had earlier, 1800, published a paper on pollen analysis in 'Transactions of the London Linnean Society' and contributed small papers or essays to other publications. But, it was largely for his (amateur) meteorological success in the classification of clouds that he was elected as a Fellow of the Royal Society in 1821. The accurate observation and simple classification was an inspiration to Goethe, who wrote a series of poems in gratitude to Howard; to John Constable in his painting of skies; to Shelley, whose poem 'The Cloud' is a description of each of Luke Howard's class of cloud.

His main profession, however, was that of a chemist. Luke Howard had his own business as chemist and druggist on Fleet Street before going into partnership, in 1797, with William Allen (the first president of the Pharmaceutical Society). Luke's role in the partnership *Allen & Howard* was the development and production of new chemicals, firstly in Plaistow and then to other premises in East London. Eventually his son, John Eliot Howard, came into the business. It continued as *Howard & Sons*, of Ilford, Essex for five generations. (The partnership *Allen & Howard* was dissolved in 1806. William Allen married Charlotte Hanbury in that year and you can probably guess the rest – it was later to become *Allen & Hanburys*, acquired in 1958 by GlaxoWellcome.)

The aforementioned are not all with which Luke Howard was actively involved, however. He, along with William Allen and other Quakers, formed the African Institution. One of its key aims was to improve the lot of African people through education. Another was to campaign for legitimate trade with Africa. It seems that Howard worked on several concerns of the time: against slavery; against Capital Punishment; against cruelty to animals; he helped to raise funds to aid

German refugees of the Napoleonic wars – for which the King of Prussia gave him a medal; and helped in the establishing of a 'Lancastrian' school.

Another Tottenham Friend was Joseph Freame. Not many people are familiar with the name today but his father, John, was a founder of the bank Freame & Gould (John married Priscilla Gould and John's sister Hannah married Thomas Gould). Freame and Gould became Freame, Gould & Barclay when, in 1733, Joseph took James Barclay into partnership, giving him a quarter share in the profits. This was Barclay's first entry into banking, until then Barclay's Cheapside Linen Drapery business was the source of their wealth. Although Barclays had not been bankers until 1733, they had joined the Freame family in 1723 when James's father, David Barclay, had married John Freame's daughter Priscilla (born circa 1700; David Barclay born 1682). Both the family and business connections were consolidated in 1733 by James Barclay's marriage to Priscilla's younger sister, Sarah Freame.

The reason for my interest in the Barclays is because they did not limit their entrepreneurial marriages to the Freames but, through the Gurneys (an even better catch than the Freames) became associated with both the Young and the Dillwyn families. The Gurneys, like the Barclays and a branch of the Staveleys, were wealthy linen merchants. They also manufactured woollens and did banking as a sideline as early as the 17th century. By about 1830 Gurneys had 20 offices whereas their competitors had only a third of that number. *Figure 47* outlines some interesting Gurney relationships.

As with all my illustrations of family, friends and acquaintances, I have been selective with the entries: John Gurney and Catherine Bell had eleven issue, not all of interest here. But, the fact that Elizabeth Gurney, who became Elizabeth Fry, was so famed for her part in prison reforms is indicative of the activity and prominence of many members of these groups of people. Also typical in this case is an apparent determination to keep all within the family, which must have been difficult sometimes without going against Quaker beliefs.

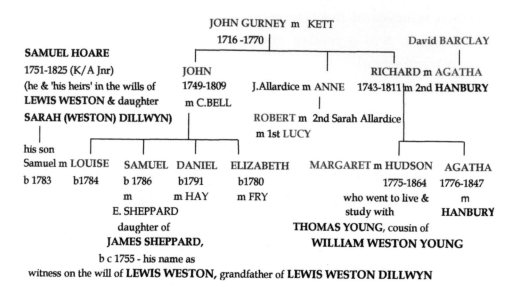

Figure 47. Some Mutual Acquaintances of the Weston (Dillwyn) and Young families. Gurney names purple, Barclay names blue

The Society of Friends, however, did not limit their friends or business acquaintances to fellow Quakers: The 'Meeting for Suffering Committee on the Slave Trade', in 1783, numbered around twenty and fewer than half of these were Quakers. Barclay and Gurney were not among the twenty or so in this particular meeting, nor were they among the smaller group to meet informally during that same year: William Dillwyn and Samuel Hoare Jnr were. (We came across Samuel Hoare in the preceding chapter.)

I now return to figure 47, in particular to Thomas Young (1773-1829), the young man who was considered, by the Gurneys, (or more particularly by David Barclay) to be an eminently suitable companion for Hudson Gurney, David Barclay's grandson. It is quite striking that it should be Hudson's grandfather to be involved in this move as it was Thomas's maternal grandfather, Robert Davis, who was largely responsible for the upbringing of and keen interest in the education of his own grandson, Thomas. 'Youngsbury' a country house in Hertfordshire, owned by the Barclay family, was where Thomas and

Hudson Gurney lived and studied together (from age 13 years and 12 years respectively).

Thomas's position within his family can be seen in *figure 48*: first cousin to William Weston Young, but through William's marriage to Thomas's aunt, Elizabeth Davis, Thomas was also William's nephew.

I referred earlier to the versatility of the intellect of Luke Howard. When it comes to Thomas Young I am lost for words, and for the appreciation he deserves I refer you to Andrew Robinson's biography of Dr Thomas Young, M.D., F.R.C.P. *'The Last Man Who Knew Everything'*.

Perhaps the thing for which he is most remembered is his work on deciphering the Rosetta Stone (a fragment of a free-standing, inscribed stone dating to 196 BC but discovered, in the Delta region of Egypt, as late as 1799). The stone can be divided into three parts; hieroglyphic script at the top, demotic script in the centre and Greek script at the bottom.

The Rev. Stephen Weston was the first person to translate the Greek script into English, which he presented to the Society of Antiquarians in London in 1802.

Thomas Young reportedly started his attempt to decipher the hieroglyphics at roughly the same time. But this was a much stiffer task and not one to which Thomas, at first, devoted his efforts; he was much occupied with the publishing of other academic studies and practising

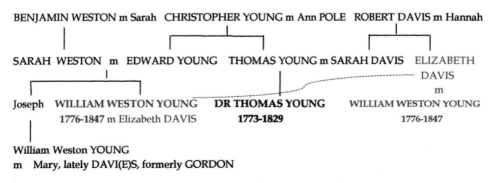

Figure 48. Dr Thomas Young's position within the family

medicine. (It should be pointed out that Thomas had left the Society some years previous. The swearing of oaths did not fit with their notion of equality and many Quakers, therefore, chose not to enter professions with that requirement. But whether or not this was the reason Thomas left the Quakers is not clear.) However, the reading of the Rosetta Stone gradually became an obsession, which, even after his initial success, he returned to at various times until he died.

In 1814, Thomas Young wrote to Hudson Gurney:

> *"You tell me that I shall astonish the world if I make out the inscription. I think it on the contrary astonishing that it should not have been made out already, and that I should find the task so difficult as it appears to be."*

Astonish the world he did, by the reasoning he applied in deciphering the hieroglyphics on no fewer than five cartouches on the Stone.

These were important achievements of Rev. Stephen Weston and particularly of Dr. Thomas Young. However, purely in the context of this book, the fact that these two people in particular were involved on the same project is of even greater importance.

Rev. Stephen Weston we have come across before (figure 29), and his brother Charles prior to that, (figure 24), on account of the close acquaintance of Charles's daughter-in-law with Anne Henrietta Weston, a witness to the marriage of William Weston's daughter Sophia. A perusal of all the *figures 24, 29, 47 and 49* will, I hope, make clear a way in which three protagonists William Weston (of the service), William Weston Young and Lewis Weston Dillwyn link.

The discovery of a Captain William Weston connected with the Weston family of the service, is significant when we consider the following information, which comes from research into possible connections between William Weston Young and Lewis Weston Dillwyn: two postscripts in the correspondence between Sir Charles

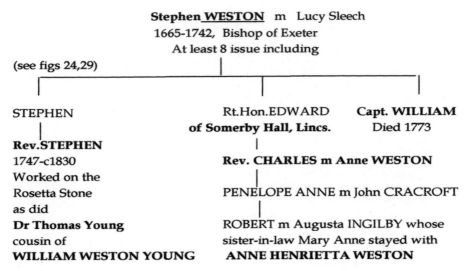

Figure 49. Another aspect of the Westons of Somerby Hall

Llewelyn and George B. Hammond refer to a Captain William Weston. Sir Charles says simply *"I can find no Capt William Weston"*. George Hammond responds with a postscript apparently in reply to that of Sir Charles's. It contains vital information but, most frustratingly, it is not fully intact and what remains is not fully legible: *figure 50* is a photocopy of the postscript. What we have is as follows:

> *Captain William Weston .*
> *was the father of the ?*....... (see fig 50 for what remains of this word)
> *of both Dr Thomas Young ...*
> *(the eminent scientist of*
> *Rosetta Stone fame) and of*
> *his Nephew W.W. Young of*
> *Swansea & Nantgarw porcelains*
> *fame*

It is a riddle I have not been able to solve. If the captain discussed in the letters is the same one now identified, then his will, written in 1766, gives no clues. The largest legacy, in the form of an annuity for life, goes to Lydia (Cooper) Horsley, a widow with whom he was living in London,

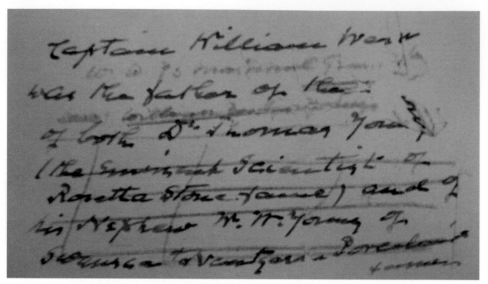

Figure 50. A Postscript regarding Captain William Weston

and a house in Devon is bequeathed to one of his nieces, Lucy Weston. Small legacies are left to all and sundry but there is no indication he has fathered any children. I can find no other Captain William Weston.

Figure 51 is another example of the intermarriages prevalent in these families. In this selection the Cox, Dillwyn and Smith names dominate, with a presence of Jones, Hill and Ellis, all of which we have met before elsewhere; and, of course, the eponymous Weston.

In relation to the marriage of George Dillwyn and Sarah Hill (*fig. 51*) it is of some interest that in 1782 Sarah's brother Henry Hill, and George Haynes were both Directors of the Bank of North America: a part of Samuel Weston's legacy to son William was in the form of monies held in the Bank of America but, more importantly, the name of George Haynes is well known in relation to the pottery in Wales – he was in partnership for a short while with William Dillwyn.

For an enlightening description of the Cambrian pottery before it was bought by William Dillwyn, and when it was run by the partnership of George Haynes and William Coles, I refer you to Jonathan Gray's account in *Welsh Ceramics in Context parts I and II*.

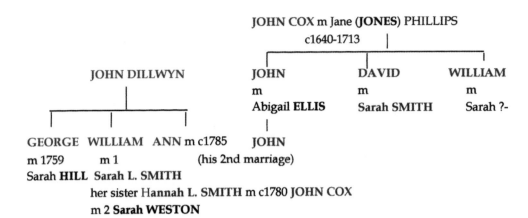

Figure 51. Intermarriage of families

Further information

The second William Weston Young (son of William Weston Young's brother Joseph, see fig 48) was born in Jamaica (circa 1798). See chapter 3 for something on the Staveleys in Jamaica; chapter 10 for the Cholmondeley reference; and further information after chapter 5 for a Davis reference.

Elizabeth Weston, spinster, the first William Weston Young's maternal aunt, made his nephew, the second William Weston Young her eventual heir.

Robert Davis (uncle of Dr Thomas Young; brother of Elizabeth and Sarah; brother-in-law of the first William Weston Young) held numerous properties. In his will of 1795 (proved 1802) Robert states of some tenanted property, "I hold by Will under Mary Wilmot".

William Weston, gentleman of Twickenham, Middlesex, in his will dated 1809, left legacies to an Elizabeth Davis and a Samuel Davis.

A William Weston made a will in 1809, before a planned return to England from Jamaica. He was a practitioner/surgeon with property in Staffordshire plus property or other financial interests in London and in America. At least two of his children in Jamaica were under 21; one son in England, William Roby Weston and wife Caroline Price Weston, had an interest in properties in St. George, Hanover Square and Stratton Street, Piccadilly (1822). John Julius William Angerstein (note his kinsman in chapter 8) and Thomas Davis had an interest in some of the same property in 1846. The extensive documents, held in London Metropolitan Archives, strongly feature the will of Joseph Price, written no later than May 1820. Sophia, was his widow by this time. Price Watkis, his nephew, was referred to in both the will of Joseph Price and that of William Weston.

Charles Van Notten married (1769) Millicent POLE. He later adopted the name of POLE. Kinsmen of Millicent Pole intermarried with STAVELEYS of Yorkshire (both previous to and later than the marriage of Millicent to Charles Van Notten.)

John Staveley of Pocklington, Yorkshire married (1745) Margaret Smeaton.

CHAPTER 10

Jane Austen's Contribution

Jane Austen was, perhaps, an unexpected name to come across in this book. The reading of Jane Austen's letters (mainly to Cassandra Austen) was supposed to provide light relief from intensive research; a distraction from the ever increasing, confusing, overlapping circles of names getting more complicated with each new document found. The letters were a good read but, as it turned out, a wrong choice for the purpose: it soon became apparent that several of the people and situations Jane Austen wrote of could be relevant to my research and could not be ignored. The results include some intricate structuring of families and property, which do not make for easy reading but are too important to omit completely.

In all truth, Jane Austen (1775-1817), though a brilliant author, could not be described as enlightened in the now peculiar application of the word for the age into which she was born. The contents of her letters reflect a keen interest in fashion and of likely romances amongst her many acquaintances, which undeniably informed her novels, and include many pertinent observations. She does also, however, give us an insight into aspects of both social and economic history.

The first extract is from a letter dated January 1801 and illustrates the complexities that can arise from the owning/leasing and releasing of a relatively simple property. It was written at Steventon and sent to Cassandra at Godmersham Park: (Le Faye, 2003)

... 'I fancy Mr Holder will have the Farm, & without being obliged to depend on the accommodating spirit of Mr William Portal; he will probably have it for the remainder of my father's lease. – This pleases us all much better than it's falling into the hands of Mr Harwood or Farmer Twitchen. – Mr Holder is to come in a day or two to talk to my father on the subject, & then John Bond's interest will not be forgotten.'...

Of the several people to have an interest in the 'Farm' Mr William Portal is the one of whom we are about to learn more. His identity is given in the biographical index of the book as William Portal (1755 -1846) of Laverstoke. Much has been written about this family and a collection of archival material is held in Hampshire Record Office.

The Portal's papermaking company of Laverstoke and Overton was founded in 1712 by Henri Portal, who was born in France of a Huguenot family. He had been naturalized as a British subject in 1711 and, with the help of his friend William Heathcote of Hursley, obtained a lease of Bere Mill. (Descendants of Sir William Heathcote, 3rd baronet of Hursley married into the families of Lovell, 1798; Bigg, 1798 – note the comparison made by Jane Austen of Catherine Bigg to the Misses Coxes, referred to in chapter 6 of this book; Lyell, 1809 and Wyndham, 1824). In 1718 Henri obtained a lease of Laverstoke Mill and by 1724 had gained a contract to make paper for Bank of England notes; the uncle of William Heathcote, Sir Gilbert Heathcote, 1st baronet of Hursley, was, at that time, Governor of the Bank of England.

It is interesting – because of the association of the porcelain trade with the East India Company – to note that Sir Gilbert (1652-1733) was a founder of the New East India Company in 1693. A junior branch of the Heathcote family settled in London.

An indication of how the Portal family was linked to the Austens is shown in *figure 52*.

Children of the next generation, that is Minnie, Ella, Constance

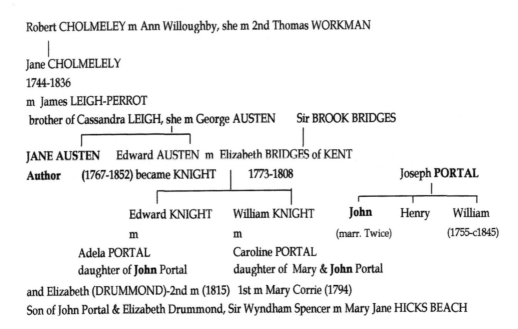

Figure 52. Austens link to Portals

and William Portal, the children of Sir Wyndham Spencer Portal and
Mary Jane (nee Hicks Beach) are shown in a photograph, taken by Mrs
Jane (Beach) St. John (unfortunately the cost of reproduction prohibits
its inclusion). The photograph is one of a collection held at Swansea
Museum, many of the photographs having been taken by Lewis Weston
Dillwyn's son John. (On coming of age, John inherited his grandfather's
estates of Penllergare and Ynysygerwn, near Swansea and assumed the
additional name of Llewelyn.) A glance at a further extract from the
family tree of Lewis Weston Dillwyn, *figure 53*, shows the inclusion of
Caroline Julia Hicks Beach and prompts a brief exposition of the Hicks
Beach family.

As might be expected, Hicks Beach is the result of the
intermarrying of the Hicks and Beach families: One such marriage
(1779) was that of Michael Hicks, of Beverston Castle and Williamstrip
Park, to Henrietta Maria Beach, daughter of William Beach of
Netheravon, Michael later becoming Hicks Beach. His elder son,
Michael Hicks Beach added Keevil Manor to the estates of this branch;

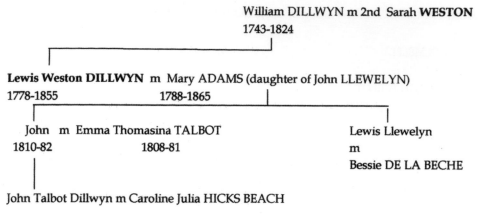

Figure 53. Small extract from the Dillwyn family tree

younger son William Hicks, later Beach, further added Oakley Hall. Other intermarriages resulted in the following combination, Hicks Hicks Beach (sensibly, the original Hicks was later dropped) and possibly numerous other combinations that need not concern us.

Caroline Julia Hicks Beach was the daughter of a Michael Hicks Beach of Beverston: Mary Jane Hicks Beach was the daughter of a William of Oakley Hall and Keevil. A slight expansion of the family of Caroline Julia (and consequently of Lewis Weston Dillwyn), *figure 54,* gives us further connections to Jane Austen but, more importantly, will take us back to William Weston of the porcelain service. We will return to this figure shortly.

Firstly, a few words on Edward Austen (c1767-1852), Jane's brother. In 1783 he was adopted by his distant cousin, Thomas Knight, and wife Catherine, of Godmersham in Kent: Godmersham Park had been the property of Knights for some time (though earlier known as Ford Park, and the proprietors often bearing other names. For example, Thomas Broadnax /Brodnax in 1727 changed his name to May – for inheritance purposes – and in 1738 adopted the name Knight, pursuant to the will of Elizabeth Knight – widow of Bulstrode Peachy Knight, but firstly married to William Knight of Dean). Thomas Knight, the son of Thomas May Knight, married Catherine Knatchbull. This is the couple who, having no expectation of children

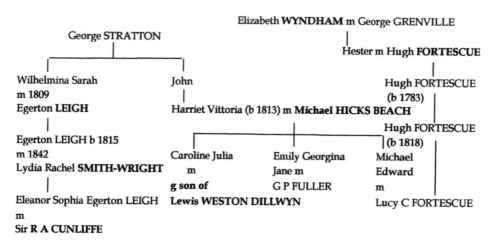

Figure 54. Cunliffe route to Dillwyns

of their own, adopted Edward Austen, who later was to change his name to Knight.

Meanwhile, the ownership of another manor in Godmersham called Eggarton was undergoing changes. Once the property of Charles, son of Sir Reginald Scott of Scotts hall, it passed on or was sold to several families during the 17th century before being devised to the daughters of William Weston/Western Hugessen of Provender; the two surviving ones being Dorothy, who married Sir Joseph Banks, and Mary, who married Edward Knatchbull. Eggarton was then sold to Thomas Knight who devised the estate and manor to Edward Austen (Knight), the said brother of Jane.

In 1791 Edward married Elizabeth Bridges, daughter of Sir Brook Bridges of Goodnestone, Kent; the names of Brook and Bridges are familiar elsewhere. That, in essence, concludes the family configurations of brother Edward.

The Austens had business with the Wedgwood factory and several mentions of Wedgwood are made by Jane in her letters, one of which refers to a service ordered by Edward. Jane is writing from Henrietta Street, London to Cassandra at Chawton on 16th September 1813:

"... We then went to Wedgwoods where my Br & Fanny chose a

Dinner Set. – I beleive (sic) *the pattern is a small Lozenge in purple, between Lines of narrow Gold; – & it is to have the Crest."*

Without sight of the service it is not known which crest was used. Two possibilities are that of Brook Bridges – 'out of a ducal coronet or, a moor's head, sa. banded ar.' (Burke 1832) – or that of Knatchbull – 'on a chapeau az. turned up erm. a leopard statant ar. spotted sa.' (Burke 1832).

We know from the description of the pattern and the date of the letter that the 'Wedgwood ware' which Jane had received in June of 1811 was something quite different. The letter was written on Thursday the 6th and on this occasion it was Jane who was at Chawton, her sister Cassandra, to whom Jane was writing, was at Godmersham Park:

"On Monday I had the pleasure of receiving, unpacking & approving our Wedgwood ware. It all came very safely, & upon the whole is a good match, tho' I think they might have allowed us rather larger leaves, especially in such a Year of fine foliage as this. One is apt to suppose that the Woods about Birmingham must be blighted. – There was no Bill with the Goods – but that shall not screen them from being paid. I mean to ask Martha to settle the account. It will be quite in her way, for she is just now sending my Mother a Breakfast set, from the same place. I hope it will come by the Waggon tomorrow; it is certainly what we want, & I long to know what it is like; & as I am sure Martha has great pleasure in making the present, I will not have any regret."

(Gaye Blake Roberts writes an interesting chapter in Gray, 2003, on an affinity of the Swansea factory with Wedgwood: she notes how extraordinary it was that four known separate travellers, in the last decade of the 18th century and first decade of the 19th century, should comment on the similarity between the Swansea factory and its wares, and the factory plan and wares of Josiah Wedgwood, indicating how closely Swansea must have been emulating Wedgwood.)

It was in 1812 that Edward adopted the name of Knight. He inherited not only the estates of Godmersham in Kent, but also Steventon and Chawton in Hampshire (Chawton House being the residence from which Jane Austen began writing her novels). However, he did not need to wait until the demise of Mrs Catherine Knight in order to have the use of her property. A letter, held in the Hampshire Record Office and dated 24 November 1797, is from Catherine Knight to Edward Austen. An abstract from the archives and describing the letter, states that it 'refers to Catherine's proposed plan to devise the estate to Edward, she sees him as an adopted child and feels for him as a mother; she believes he will be happy and hopes to be near enough to visit daily'.

Jane Austen did not greet Mrs Knight's plan regarding the property in Godmersham, Kent, with much gratitude. An extract from a letter she wrote from Steventon to Cassandra at Godmersham, in early January, 1799 illustrates her view:

> *"Mrs Knights giving up the Godmersham Estate to Edward was no such prodigious act of Generosity after all it seems, for she has reserved herself an income out of it still; – this ought to be known, that her conduct may not be over-rated. – I think Edward shews the most Magnanimity of the two, in accepting her Resignation with such Incumbrances."*

The year of the letter from Mrs Knight to Edward, 1797, was an interesting one in another respect. It was the year in which the section of the Kennet and Avon canal between Kintbury and Newbury was opened. The chairman of the Kennet & Avon Canal Company was Charles Dundas, the Dundas family being squires of Kintbury. Thomas, the son of Reverend Thomas Fowle of Kintbury had been engaged to Cassandra Austen, but sadly died of fever in the West Indies when there as chaplain to his relative, Lord Craven.

Samuel Weston, father of William, had played a part in the section of the Kennet and Avon canal from Newbury to Bath. He, along with

Samuel Simcock and James Barnes made surveys for narrow and barge canals for this section, late in 1788 (Shead).

The canal was used by the Austens (at least was the stretch from Hungerford to Chawton) but, judging from the tone of the following extract, not with relish. Again, the letter was to Cassandra, addressed to the Post Office at Cheltenham, and written from Chawton over 2 days, 8th and 9th September, 1816 and refers, in part, to her reply to Charles about his planned visit to Chawton. It is an extended extract, to include a somewhat Dickensian (though a forerunner and, perhaps, less sympathetic) approach to the vagrant fortunes of families:

"...When you have once left Cheltenham, I shall grudge every half day wasted on the road. If there were but a coach from Hungerford to Chawton! – I have desired him to let me hear again soon. – He does not include a Maid in the list to be accomodated (sic), *but if they bring one, as I suppose they will, we shall have no bed in the house even then for Charles himself – let alone Henry – . But what can we do? – We shall have the Gt House quite at our command; – it is to be cleared of the Papillons Servants in a day or two; – they themselves have been hurried off into Essex to take possession – not of a large Estate left them by an Uncle – but to scrape together all they can I suppose of the effects of a Mrs Rawstorn a rich old friend & cousin, suddenly deceased, to whom they are joint Executors. So, there is a happy end of the Kentish Papillons coming here."*
(Note the further information at the end of the chapter)

Before we leave the area of Newbury, there is a tale to tell of Henry Bridges, 2nd Duke of Chandos. James Leigh, the uncle of Cassandra (Leigh) Austen and, therefore, great uncle to Jane Austen, married Lady Caroline Brydges, daughter of the said Henry Bridges, 2nd Duke of Chandos. (The difference in the spellings of Bridges is confusing: the family can be traced back to the 15th century when the patronym was Brugge but some of the issue appear as Brydges. By the 16th century some families have the patronym Brydges with some issue appearing as Bridges. The example of Lady Caroline and Henry is the reverse.)

The story goes as follows: Henry was journeying to London and stopped to dine at the Pelican Inn in Newbury. Whilst at the inn a commotion broke out in the yard. The cause of the noise was the pending sale by the inn's ostler of his wife, Anne, daughter of John Wells of Newbury and St. Marylebone. She was being led into the yard with a halter around her neck. Henry reportedly fell in love with Anne on the spot and bought her. Henry's wife died in 1738, the ostler in 1744. Henry married the ostler's widow and she became Anne, Duchess of Chandos. I cannot vouch for the authenticity of all details of the tale, but it is well established that Henry did marry Anne.

Henry's Aunt, Mary Brydges (sister to 1st Duke/9th Baron Chandos of Sudeley), married Theophilus Leigh and Henry's daughter, Lady Caroline Brydges, married James Leigh, whose relationship to Jane Austen is given above.

The lineage to the peerages associated with the (Goodneston, Kent) Brook-Bridges family of the early 18th and early 19th centuries is clear (Burke 1832). The same cannot be said of the lineage associated with the Chandos peerage: a claim to the barony of Chandos was made in 1789 by the Rev. Edward Tymewell Brydges, urged to do so by his younger brother Sir Samuel Egerton Brydges (1762-1837). Hearings of the case before the committee of privileges of the House of Lords began the following year, 1790, and continued until 1803, when it was finally decided that no claim to the title and dignity of Baron Chandos had been proved.

Samuel Egerton Brydges, the prime mover of the Chandos Peerage case, was a known literary figure. He was more respected for his non-fictional works, which included an enlarged edition of Collins's 'Peerage of England' in nine volumes, published in 1812, than for his poetry and novels, though they were not without some commercial success. Jane Austen's father bought a copy of the novel *Arthur Fitz-Albini*, published in 1798. A letter written from Jane, at Steventon, late November 1798, to her sister Cassandra, staying with brother Edward at Godmersham, reveals her opinion of the novel:

"We have got 'Fitz-Albini'; my father has bought it against my private wishes, for it does not quite satisfy my feelings that we should purchase the only one of Egerton's works of which his family are ashamed. That these scruples, however, do not at all interfere with my reading it, you will easily believe. We have neither of us yet finished the first volume. My father is disappointed – I am not, for I expected nothing better. Never did any book carry more internal evidence of its author. Every sentiment is completely Egerton's. There is very little story, and what there is told in a strange, unconnected way. There are many characters introduced, apparently merely to be delineated. We have not been able to recognise any of them hitherto, except Dr and Mrs Hey and Mr Oxenden, who is not very tenderly treated."

(It was recognized that the novel freely depicted foibles of family and relations of Samuel Egerton Brydges, as well as other acquaintances, which may have been one of the reasons his family were ashamed of the work.)

Earlier in this chapter a return to figure 54 was promised. The figure was included, in the first instance, to illustrate some mutual family connections of Jane Austen and Lewis Weston Dillwyn. Now, the same figure takes us around to William Weston.

We have Eleanor Sophia Egerton Leigh, of Cheshire, to thank; for she married Sir Robert Alfred Cunliffe (born 1839). Eleanor Sophia came from stock already familiar to us; her father was Egerton Leigh and her mother Lydia Rachel Smith Wright, daughter of John Smith Wright of Nottingham (see chapter 7 and figure 30). Robert Alfred was the grandson of the Sir Foster Cunliffe (1755-1834), with whom we are now familiar as a person linked to Samuel Weston (father of William Weston) in the Brooke family papers.

Before summarizing the Austen family connections, there are further veins to tap. The richest sources again come from the maternal side of Jane Austen's family.

Jane's uncle, James Leigh, benefitted from the circumstances of generous relatives and his own position in the family in much the same way as did Jane's brother Edward Austen (Knight). James Leigh's mother's maiden name was Perrot; when his spinster great aunt, Ann Perrot was about to inherit the fortune and Oxfordshire estate of her childless brother Thomas, she asked that James Leigh inherit all instead, excepting an annuity for herself. Thomas Perrot agreed, on the condition that James adopt the name of Perrot.

Thomas Perrot died 1751. Consequently, it was as James Leigh-Perrot that James married Jane Cholmeley in 1764.

Mrs Jane (Cholmeley) Leigh-Perrot became a public figure when, in Bath in the summer of 1799, she was accused of picking up (stealing) some white lace along with her purchase of black lace. At the trial, which took place at Taunton assizes the following March, Mrs Leigh-Perrot was found 'Not-Guilty'. The case has been widely written of and debated. Public opinion seems somewhat divided; one explanation given for the verdict, by those who did not believe her innocence, is that, because of the value attributed to the lace, the death penalty could have been 'too harsh' a punishment if she had been found guilty. Though, in fact, transportation would have been more likely. Because of the social position of Mrs Jane (Cholmeley) Leigh Perrot, the intervening months between the charge and the trial were spent in the home of the gaol-keeper of Somerset County Gaol, rather than in the gaol. By all accounts, Mr Scadding and family did all they could to make the stay of their honoured guests, Mr and Mrs Leigh-Perrot (for James stayed close by his beloved wife), as comfortable as possible. But, the *"Vulgarity, Dirt, Noise from Morning till Night"* of which Jane Leigh-Perrot wrote, obviously made it impossible for her to *'enjoy'* the accommodation provided. To be fair, it was not the personal affront but the subjection of her husband to such things that Jane Leigh Perrot claimed caused her the greatest misery. She expanded on this in her letter to relatives in Lincolnshire:

"Cleanliness has ever been his greatest delight and yet he sees the

greasy toast laid by the dirty Children on his Knees, and feels the
small Beer trickle down his sleeves on its way across the table
unmoved ... Mrs Scadding's Knife well licked to clean it from fried
onions helps me now and then".

It was the Cholmeley relatives in Easton, Lincolnshire, to whom
Mrs Leigh-Perrot wrote but Lord Cholmondeley, of the related Cheshire
branch, who corresponded, through his agent, (1800) with 'Mr Weston',
then of Oxford (as noted in chapter 7). It may be remembered that
Samuel Weston was originally from Cheshire

Sir Richard Cholmondeley (1472-1521) used that particular
spelling of the name, although his father, John, is recorded as
Cholmeley. Sir Richard was born in Cheshire but moved, when very
young to Yorkshire and eventually held estates or properties in several
locations including Northumberland, Essex, Middlesex, London and
Kent. Sir Richard's nephew, Richard Cholmeley (son of his brother
Roger) is the line from which the Lincolnshire Cholmeleys descend. Sir
Richard's   cousin,   Richard   Cholmondeley   remained   as   'of
Cholmondeley', Cheshire.

Jane Cholmeley was born in Barbados, where, as well as in
Jamaica, her father Robert had interests (chapter 3 gives information
on the Staveleys in Jamaica; notes at the end of this chapter and of
chapters 5 and 9 give other Caribbean links). But she was returned to
England for her schooling and was watched over by Robert's brother
John, of Lincolnshire. John's son Montague was a particular Cholmeley
relative with whom Jane kept in touch.

The importance of a reminder of the further information at the end of chapter
7 regarding Montague Cholmeley necessitates an interruption to the natural
flow of this passage, for which I apologize.

Another useful Leigh connection is that to the Egerton family. There
was a clue that such a marriage had taken place in the name Egerton
Leigh, figure 54, which took us to the significant Cunliffe marriage.

It is necessary to recite more of this family tree, tedious though it may be to the reader, because it draws our key players closer together: Direct ancestors of Egerton Leigh were Peter Leigh, rector of Lymm and Whitchurch, who married Elizabeth, daughter of Thomas Egerton of Tatton Park. Elizabeth's niece, Hester Egerton, married William Tatton of Wythenshaw (his mother was Hannah Wright). Paradoxically, their son, William Tatton (1749-1806), later changed his name to Egerton in order to inherit Tatton Park – obviously other Egerton/Tatton combinations pre-date this one but we do not need to identify them. The key marriage, in the context of this book, is that in 1773, of the latter named William Tatton *Egerton* to Frances Maria Fountayne, daughter of John Fountayne DD, Dean of York (1715 – 1802).

The Very Reverend John Fountayne was brother to Anne, the second wife of the Rt. Hon. Edward Weston of Somerby Hall, Lincolnshire, whose connections to William Weston of the service and to William Weston Young are delineated in figures 24, 29, 49.

A justification for including the family of Jane Austen in this book, if one were needed, is summarized in the connections (not necessarily all familial ones) shown in *figure 55*.

Lastly, as the Westons of most significance in relation to William Billinglsey all feature in the preceding figure, it would be remiss not to include in this chapter the Weston family of Cranbrooke, Kent; the family, shown in *figure 56*, is, perhaps, the closest familial link of Weston to Austen yet described. John Austen, of Broadford, and Thomas Knight, of Godmersham, are given bequests and named as executors in the will of John Weston of Cranbrooke, dated 1754 and proved in 1765 after his death.

Further information

Some Caribbean plantations were described as of Cholmeley, Workman ownership. A letter in the Derbyshire archives confirms that Thomas Workman was still in Barbados in 1772.

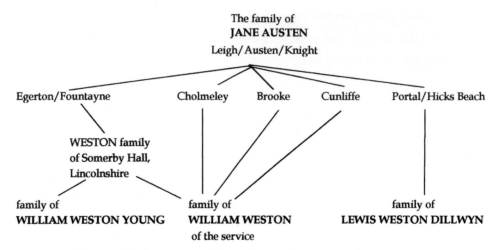

Figure 55. Summary of Jane Austen links to our protagonists

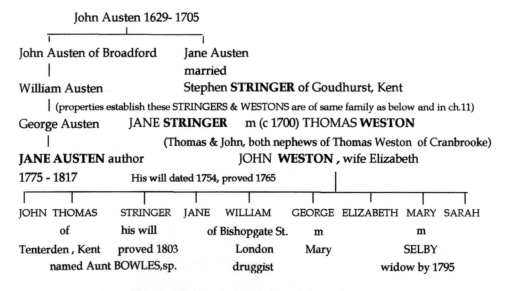

Figure 56. Weston cousins of Jane Austen

*Note the marriage of Sophronia/Sophronica Weston to a S. Workman, figure
57.*

A few other marriages of possible interest:

(i)   *Rev. Thomas Egerton m (1836) Charlotte Catherine Milner*

(ii)   *Hon. Alice Mary Egerton m (1867) Reginald Cholmondeley, son of Rev.*
        Charles Cowper Cholmondeley (the sister of Alice Mary, Emily
        Marianne, through her marriage to Percy Mitford, became connected to
        the Wright family of figure 30)

(iii) *Marriage settlement, c1698, Edward Knatchbull and Alice Wyndham.*

A_2A *London Metropolitan Archives, Chandos family papers names a Peter*
        Waldo as an interested party, alongside Francis Brydges, in the marriage
        settlement of the intended marriage of James Brydges and Cassandra
        Willoughby, 1713. (See chapter one for a Peter Waldo/Samuel Billingsley
        connection.)

A_2A *Lincolnshire archives, Jarvis (first referred to at the end of chapter one,*
        in relation to Samuel Billingsley) gives an 'acknowledgment by David
        and Esther Papillon that James Gunman, as trustee of their marriage
        settlement had received £50 for sale of a piece of land to William Deede of
        Hythe and had given it to David Papillon'.

David Papillon of Acrise & Lee, Kent, married (as his second wife) Esther,
        daughter of Rev. Doctor Curteis of Sevenoaks, Kent.

This David Papillon is a descendant of Thomas Papillon who had married Jane,
        daughter of Thomas Broadnax of Godmersham.

Still with the same Jarvis papers, there are many documents relating to
        Margaret Blackwell, sister-in-law of G.R.P. Jarvis. In addition, Margaret
        Blackwell has documents in the papers of Knollis/Knollys (Earls of
        Banbury) family, held in the Hampshire record office: Margaret was the
        sister of Charlotte Knollys. These documents, which run from 1662 to
        1836, include many fascinating letters ranging from peerage claims to
        the Gordon riots. Some, circa 1812, under the documents of William
        Knollis, 8ᵗʰ Earl, tell of the imminent demise of Margaret's brother John
        and request the attendance of Margaret and "his" sisters – whose sisters
        is not clear from the abstract. A subsequent letter questions the bill
        received for their visit; coachman and horses, accommodation and food:
        this is followed by further questioning of the bill for the man and horses
        and refers to a Mr Wickham. These are not the most fascinating of the
        letters but are noted because of the character Mr Wickham in Jane

Austen's novel 'Pride and Prejudice'; just one name among many I have come across that can be found in her novels – including D'Arcy: these have generally been ignored, concentrating on the facts not her fiction, but perhaps this one exception will be forgiven.

A$_2$A Oxfordshire, Bradwell Grove Estate (Hey), 1812, 1 item: Parties include John Webbe Weston late of Sutton Place, Surrey, now of Bath. Subject of Transaction – Manor of Lordship of Holwell, such parts as are not comprised in the term of 200yrs by Indenture of Release of 8 July 1653. It includes John Wright (of Kelvedon Hall), Thomas Wells, Widow Baker, **Mary Adams**. (Earlier similar items in the papers – early 18th century – feature Perrott, Brookes and Hampson.)

CHAPTER 11

An Aside: Was Miriam Weston of Sound Mind?

The Westons referred to at the close of the previous chapter (fig. 56) are kinsmen of the Weston family featured in the Chancery case of *Weston con Weston and Weston* (National Archives, Kew), whose members are outlined in *figure 57*.

The cause of Chancery was a dispute over the will of Miriam Weston, dated 11th December 1848 and, in particular, the codicil dated the same day. A further codicil was added 17th January 1849.

The will extends to six pages but the extracts given below give the gist of the content:

> *This is the last Will and Testament of me Miriam Weston of North End Terrace, Fulham, Middlesex, widow ... my executrixes and trustees ... shall purchase of the trustees of the Family Settlement ... in the year one thousand eight hundred and twenty, six cottages ... near Cranbrook in the County of Kent in the same settlement mentioned for as much money as they are fairly worth and ... convey the said cottages unto my granddaughters Louisa Clifford Miriam Sedgwick and Ann Oyler and their heirs ...*
>
> *I direct ... to pay such a sum of money as should be equal to what a farm called ?Beach/Breech Farm also ... in the said settlement together with the timber thereon and all appurtenant thereunto*

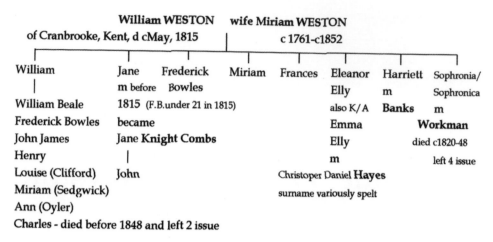

Figure 57. Miriam Weston's family tree

shall be sold ... one fifth unto each of my grandchildren William Beal Weston Frederick Bowles Weston John James Weston Henry Weston and one fifth to the two children of my late grandson Charles Weston ... if any of my said grandsons shall die ... children alive ... shall take among them the one fifth share their father would have taken ... And I request ... trustees ... give my grandson William Beale Weston the first option of purchasing the said farm ... at a fair valuation ...

And inasmuch as by the said Settlement the sum of one thousand pounds ... to be set apart in trust for my daughter Jane Knight Combs and her children and the residue of the monies ... settled upon my other five daughters ?Sophronia (since deceased) Miriam Harriett Frances and Eleanor Elly and their children in equal shares ... but (if it does) *not turn out to be equal to one thousand pounds apiece I direct my executrixes in such case to advance out of my estate sufficient money to make up the shares ...*

And as to all the Rest and Residue of my estate ... I give ...upon the trusts ... namely one equal sixth part thereof to divide and pay the same amongst the four children of my deceased daughter ?Sophronia Workman ... to pay one other equal sixth part unto my daughter Miriam ... and one other ... unto my daughter Frances ...

And upon further trust to invest the remaining three sixth parts on Government or real securities or Parliamentary Funds of Great Britain ... as to one of the three ... to pay the dividends ... into the proper hands of my daughter Jane Knight Combs ... as to one of the other said three ... to pay the dividends ... into the proper hands of my daughter Harriot Banks ... as to the remaining share to permit my said daughter Emma Elly wife of Christopher Daniel Hayes ... the same ...

... if any person or persons benefitted by this my Will shall institute any suit at Law or in Equity or raise any dispute or demand whatsoever concerning the estate of my late husband ... or ... execution of this Will or ... concerning the non-performance or non execution of the trusts ... or concerning any sum or sums of money which have been or ought to have been received ... then the benefit or share and interest under this my will of such person or persons shall be forfeited ... and if either of my sons in law shall so offend it shall be taken to be the act of his wife and children ...

And I appoint my daughters Miriam Weston and Frances Weston executrixes and trustees of this my will and I hereby revoke all former wills by me at any time made In witness whereof I have ... set my hand this eleventh day of December in the year of our Lord one thousand eight hundred and forty eight – (signed M Weston) *... in the presence of us present at the same time ... our names as witnesses* (signed Sophia Brown Servant to M[rs] Weston – Henry Topp Clerk to ?Mess[es] Scott & Combs St Mildred Court London)

Whereas I have since making my will had reason to alter my mind concerning my grandsons John James Weston and Henry Weston Now I do hereby revoke the bequest to them of one fifth apiece of the sum at which the ?Beach Farm shall be sold for and direct that the said two fifths shall fall into the residue of my estate and be held by my executrixes upon the trusts in my will ... Witness my hand this eleventh day of December one thousand eight hundred and

Figure 58. The Momentous Interview by H.K. Browne

Figure 59. In Conference by H.K. Browne

Figure 60. Bearer of Evil Tidings by H.K. Browne

forty eight – (signed M Weston) *Signed by the ?testatrise as a Codicil to her Will in the presence of us present at the same time ...* (signed Sophia Brown – Henry Topp)

I Miriam Weston do give to my daughters Miriam and Frances all the household furniture with the linen and plate belonging to me – (signed Miriam Weston.) *... subscribed our names as*

witnesses (signed Miriam Weston – Jane ?Butler/Buller –
Sophia Brown Servant to Mrs Weston) *17 Jany 1849*

> *In the Prerogative Court of Canterbury*
>
> *In the Goods of Miriam Weston Widow deceased*
>
> *Appeared Personally Jane ?Butler/Buller of No 1 North End
> Terrace ... Spinster ... one of the subscribed witnesses to the second
> and last Codicil to the last will ... of Miriam Weston formerly of
> Edward Square Kensington but late of North End Terrace ...
> further made oath that the said words name and date were so
> written at the end of the said codicil by Frances Weston Spinster the
> daughter of the deceased ... (signed Jane ?Butler/Buller) – On
> the seventeenth day of May one thousand eight hundred and fifty
> two ...*
>
> *Proved at London with two codicils 20th May 1852 ... by the oaths
> of Miriam Weston and Frances Weston ...*

It will come as no surprise to the reader that 'Mr John Weston', in
a conversation with Sophia Brown recorded in Chancery, *"expressed that
he had been cut out of Mrs Weston's will very improperly he thought"*.

But before the story of this will (revealed through the affidavits of
witnesses) begins proper, a little more information should be added to
that provided by Miriam in her will:

We learn from the will of William Weston of Cranbrooke, dated
3rd March 1815 (proved May 1815 after his death), that, in addition to
the six daughters also mentioned in the later will of Miriam, he had a
son William Weston and son Frederick Bowles Weston.

Seemingly, Jane was the only daughter married at the time. The
fact that William appoints Peter Wm Smith (of Reading, Berkshire) and
Thomas Weston guardians for his children, 'at the death of his wife',
suggests some were of a young age. Certainly Frederick was under
twenty-one.

Son William was left only fifty pounds. The will followed on with

"... the reason why I do not give him greater benefit under this Will

is because I consider him already provided for ..."

In his will, William refers to his dear wife (and sole executrix) as Marian and to one of his daughters as Marianne. However, in the codicil (dated 11th March 1815), in which he gives his sole executrix the full power to sell and dispose of any of his estates except the old Mansion house left to Frederick Bowles Weston, the executrix is referred to as Miriam. And Miriam subsequently refers to a daughter as Miriam, with no mention of a Marianne. This rather loose use of names is by no means unusual but of no help to research.

The question of whether Miriam Weston was of sound mind when she wrote her will and codicils is one which is raised in the eighty three pages of a bound volume of depositions of 1852 (statements taken mostly in July). The answer is left to the judgment of the reader.

An account of circumstances surrounding the will is given, in varying lengths, by Henry Topp, clerk at the firm of Scott and Combs, of which Miriam Weston's grandson John Comb/s is a principal; John Combs himself; Sophia Brown, servant to the same Miriam Weston and Jane Butler/Buller an acquaintance of long standing and more recently a neighbour of Miriam's.

Henry Topp witnessed the signing of the will and first codicil. This took place at Mrs Weston's home, near the Hammersmith Gate at Fulham, where, he states, he was let into the house by Miss Frances Weston. He recalls that Mrs Weston made a remark respecting two of her grandsons William James and Henry *"... they shall have none of my money – they have offended me"*. Henry later signs another statement correcting the names: he says he made a mistake and that she said 'John James'. Although he is aware that Mr Combs has an interest in the will in question through his mother, Henry confirms that he is not himself related or indebted.

The reliability of Henry Topp's statement is put in some doubt; firstly by the critical wrong naming of a grandson who was eventually excluded from the will.; secondly, there are some points on which his statement does not agree with that made by Sophia Brown, though in this respect we have to judge which of them is more likely to be correct.

Sophia states that Miss Frances Weston was away from home on the day of the will signing. Frances could not, therefore, have let Henry into the house.

Henry claims that Mrs Weston was present when the first codicil was written, Sophia says otherwise.

Sophia Brown was the only person to witness all three documents – the will plus two codicils. She left the employ of Mrs Weston in February 1849 after four and a half years in her service. It was Sophia who ascribed an age (90, or near 90) to Mrs Weston at the time of her death. In her statement she tells us that:

> *"When Miss Weston* (Miriam) *had told me beforehand that I was to sign a paper or 'the will' I told her I would rather have nothing to do with it ... for I thought it not unlikely that it might lead to some disputes for she and her mother was so given to disagree ... there was such frequent wrangling between her and her mother"* Sophia recalled that Mrs M Weston had said she *"'wanted some little alteration' Mr Combs told her it was too late unless she had a fresh will made and she sayed 'never mind'"* In answer to the question of the state of mind of Mrs Weston, Sophia *"... cannot say ...(she was) ... in her right mind. I refer to her not letting her daughter have but hardly any fire and her coming sometimes and taking off half the kitchen fire when I was cooking ... ... she was quiet enough the day the will was signed"* She later comes back to this topic. *"I cannot say that Mrs Weston was not of sound mind (as much at least as she ever was)"*.

It was, of course, when Sophia was with a new master that she was called upon to make a statement. Evidently she had made one statement prior to the extracts quoted above, as she goes on to describe the first approach. Her new master (not named) had directed her to accompany Mr Combs to the office of Mr Denne and Mr Jellicoe. Later

Miss Frances Weston and her sister Mrs Hays had called and told her they had heard of her visit to ?Deveton Commons and commented that they should have been obliged if Sophia had let them know. One of them had remarked that they *"should be left without a shilling"*. Sophia stated she had told them (it is not clear whether 'them' refers to Denne and Jellicoe or Frances and her sister) that she *"considered that Miss Weston had influence over her mother at different times – though I did not know that she influenced her about the will"*. She had gone to the office of Denne and Jellicoe with her sister (who, incidentally, had been with Mrs Miriam Weston for eleven years prior to Sophia taking up the position) and reports *"Mr Combes sayed my expenses would be paid and Mr Denne ... gave my sister and me half a sovereign each – though we neither of us wished for anything of the kind."*

Sophia reiterates the claim that Mrs Miriam Weston was, particularly as she got older, much under the influence of Misses Frances and Miriam, especially Miriam. And later states *"... Miriam Weston would get over the deceased in almost anything by a little management"*. It was this daughter who had offered her *"a glup of wine"* as she had felt nervous about signing the will, but she had declined. At this point, Sophia was quick to stress her superior moral fibre by noting that Tealy, a servant who lived next door had had a *"Glup of wine – or gin"* when she had to sign something and was nervous.

Jane Butler/Buller, a 55 year old spinster and neighbour of Mrs Weston's for the past 18–20 years, first met the deceased and her daughters when they were living in Edward's Square. She witnessed only the second codicil and, therefore, has little to add of importance to the content of the will and first codicil; save two questions regarding the general propriety of the drawing up of the documents: Jane notes that Mrs Weston signed without wearing her spectacles and questions when some of the content may have been written; she recalls something being said about putting in the date later and Mrs Weston saying *"Yes do my dear"*.

It is interesting that Miriam did not wear her spectacles when signing the second codicil. We do not know the time of day of that signing but, according to John Combs (aged 35 years in 1852), the will itself was read by daylight and signed by candlelight – about four o'clock. John Combs's comments support Sophia Brown's observation that Mrs Weston was under the influence of her daughter, Miriam, but says that it was on domestic, unimportant things.

The will of 1848 was not the first to have been drawn up for Miriam by her grandson. He had acted for her since 1840, when he prepared her will and a codicil to that will in 1842. In 1848, Miriam, his aunt, had come to his office in St. Mildred's Court and said Mrs Miriam Weston had determined the will should not stand and that she had torn it up (whether it had actually been torn up was later brought into question). A reason given was that an executor, Reverend Peter French, had intimated he would not act. (Would a change of executor warrant a total rewriting of a will? Probably not.) Later we will come to claims of other reasons for changing the will.

Following the visit from his Aunt Miriam, John Combs and his clerk Henry Topp called to see Mrs Weston at her home. Combs cannot recollect whether or not it was by appointment. He does recall, however, the need to send Topp to get a sheet of paper at Hammersmith – Combs had forgotten 'one in which to envelope the will' – whilst he went on to his grandmother's home alone. He also confirms that on his arrival he found his mother (Mrs Weston's daughter, Jane Knight Combs) sitting with his grandmother and states that it was "... *quite a surprise to me finding my mother there*".

There were no statements to corroborate his version of the early part of the interview but he relayed the following outcomes, as he remembered them.

> *"The general scheme of her instructions was in the first instance to get rid as it were of her grandchildren, the children of her late son William* (the will refers only to daughter Sophronia and grandson Charles having died. In view of the will of his father in 1815, William would not be expected to feature in the will whether still living or not, so this reference cannot

be accepted as a full confirmation of his death) ... *and divide it* (the property and money) *between her daughters and their children ..." "no doubt I asked her 'Now Miriam, what will you do first and what will you do next ... and what will you do with the rest of your property' and so on ..." "I recollect that when she mentioned the cottages I did not feel sure, knowing that my father had bought several cottages ... ... on settlement ..."*

Combes said he asked Frances to produce the original will. There was no claim at this stage that it had, in fact, been torn up.

The statement of John Combs goes on to say he:

"was aware from communications with my grandmother that she was disposed to think that her former will was too stringent ... especially as regarded her other unmarried daughter Miss Frances Weston ... 'I think Frances should have her money as well as Miriam'..."

On 1.12.1848 he had *"had tea with my grandmother and two aunts"* and had taken notes for the new will. He then itemizes bequests, in essence much the same as appear in Miriam's will, but four of the lines have been altered, they are very confused and the sequence of those lines is hard to decipher. Those lines follow on with *"Her directions were, as it had been in her previous will I think ..."* ... *"I noted down from her dictation the names of her said grandchildren ... a few observations passed between us as to one of her grandsons Charles being dead, and his share going to his two children* (he later says that he does not know the names of these, the two children of Charles Weston, deceased son of William Weston) ... He confirms here that the indication that the earlier will had been destroyed had been a mistake and *"it turned out to be the codicil."*

More details as to the distribution of the estates are given and then an explanation of *"the clause 'as to going to law' ...cutting off any of her family who should file a bill or otherwise take any legal steps in reference to the settlement"* was because this line of action was *"supposed to have been contemplated by some Branch of the family"*.

John Combs's version of his grandmother saying, on the eleventh of December, 1848 *"John and Henry will have none of my property ..."* was similar to that of Henry Topp's. He did not know from his grandmother why she had cut out her grandsons but said *"I conjectured in my own mind what was the cause"*. Unfortunately, he does not expand on this. What was said next by him differs from Sophia Brown's account. According to Combs he said that it *"would need a codicil"* and denies saying that it was too late and would need another will.

In addition to his affidavit, there was included as evidence, a letter written by Combs to his grandmother after a visit, though precisely to what he refers and when the course of action he refers to was decided upon, is not clear: *"...this course appears to me in a legal and practical point of view much preferable to the other course ... some of them being abroad and one dead leaving infant children ... other course would necessarily lead to trouble and expense and the incurring of responsibility in taking security ..."*

He insists in his statement that he acted scrupulously. He was paid five sovereigns for his work in drawing up the will. As to how much he benefitted from the revisions, John Combs states *"The deceased's personal estate is I believe of the value of somewhere about £22,000 – but I have no knowledge on the point"*. And he concludes that the new will/codicil will make a difference of about £15 to him.

I have not found the judgement of this dispute.

CHAPTER 12

Ceramic Bodies

It is time to take a step away from characters and to the subject of ceramics, before considering the 'Weston service' in more detail.

Although I have something of a scientific background, my knowledge and understanding of the complexities surrounding various ceramic bodies is extremely limited: it is one of those subjects that, as you learn a little, you realize you know even less than you thought you did. Also, an effort to condense complexities invariably leads to statements that are not strictly accurate. In spite of its shortcomings, this short chapter is included as background for readers who may have come to this book from an angle other than ceramics.

We start with the basic premise that porcelain is translucent and pottery opaque. It does not apply in every single instance but it holds well in general terms. Another distinction is that porcelain is non-porous and earthenware pottery remains porous. These are characteristics applied to the final products, but the intrigues lie in how such differences come to be: it is no surprise that at the outset of experiments to produce porcelain, outside of China, porcelain was sometimes referred to as white gold and alchemists were called upon to find the key.

The principle characteristics of ceramic wares are affected by the recipe and the temperature at which the products are fired: they are determined by the temperatures at which various components melt into their liquid phase; precipitate crystals; and hold together small particles when the products are cooled. In general, the higher the temperature that is reached; the longer it is kept at that temperature then the more translucent, the stronger and less porous will be the final products.

Petuntse (china stone) and kaolin (china clay) are the basic components used in the porcelain referred to as hard paste or, more in past times than today, as 'true' porcelain. Other porcelains can go under a variety of names, soft paste and 'artificial' being the early commonly used descriptions. Different clays; additional ingredients in a range of proportions; firings under varying conditions, together form the basis of experimental porcelain up to the standard type of bone china in use today.

A couple of other factors in porcelain production are worth a mention: firstly, a fluxing agent is usually added. This is an ingredient that lowers the temperature at which the melting phase of production can take place. Again in general terms, the higher the clay content in relation to flux and a thinning agent (which may be used to reduce the level of shrinkage) the harder the paste; conversely, the lower the clay content in relation to flux and thinner, the softer the paste. Secondly, according to the levels of iron in the clay, the resulting product after firing may be yellow, reddish brown or brown. In kaolin, iron is replaced by aluminium, hence a white clay.

The advantages of hard paste are apparent; strong, non-porous, and a whiteness that suggests purity and sophistication. But soft paste has its advantages too; it produces a surface that lends itself to superior decoration – at lower firing temperatures more colours can withstand the heat, thus a greater choice is available for use by the ceramic artist. Plus, the slightly more porous body allows the paint to 'sink in' slightly, giving a warmer effect favoured by some. (The latter property may be affected by the glaze used; another complexity.)

William Billingsley, it seems, was looking for the best of both worlds. He wanted to have the advantages of soft paste, for his palette, without losing the advantages of hard paste: this was achieved, exemplified by

Figure 61. A Nantgarw plate

much of the porcelain produced at Nantgarw (note, in *figure 61*, the visibility of the stand through the porcelain, illustrating the even and high translucency of this Nantgarw porcelain plate). However, as was noted in the first chapter, the instability of the porcelain in firing meant that the kiln losses were great, making this fine porcelain a poor commercial product.

Examination of pieces that have failed in the kiln can give an indication of the cause of the failure. To this end, Owen et al, 1998, examined the composition of shards from Nantgarw (ten) and from Swansea (nine), but acknowledged the limitation that unless a particular flaw is present in the shard being investigated, the precise nature of the firing problem may elude recognition. It was stated, however, that historical documents suggest a common cause of failure of Billingsley's porcelain related to "shivering" (sagging or distortion) of the paste – predominantly a phosphatic paste (one that contained a proportionately large amount of bone ash); described as essentially an 18th century product carried through to the 19th century. An example of a cup that has sagged below the handle is shown in *figure 62*.

An important finding by Owen et al (1998) was that two types of recipes, phosphatic and silicious, appear to have been used at both of the manufactories under investigation: the silicious type was previously unknown amongst Nantgarw wares and differed from other, also less phosphatic (soapstone type) porcelains produced at Swansea (one respect in which it was found to differ was in the relative

Figure 62. Sagged cup

proportions of Aluminium compounds). Unfortunately, the shards could not be dated so it is not known whether the silicious recipe was ever tried in the first Nantgarw period, or if only after having been first tried at Swansea.

Out of the ten Nantgarw samples only one was silica rich; one was an in-between, described as silicious phosphatic; and the remaining eight were phosphatic. Of the nine Swansea samples only one was phosphatic.

The one phosphatic Swansea shard is of particular interest as it is from the Biddulph dinner and dessert service, first referred to in chapter 7 (in that instance because of the Soame/Myddleton/Biddulph connection to the Westons). It should be noted that the phosphatic Nantgarw shards were found to be compositionally distinct from the phosphatic porcelain of the Biddulph service.

One last point to note regarding the extensive Biddulph service is that some pieces are attributed to the Swansea porcelain factory, decorated in London, and others to Coalport. *Figure 63* shows some plates from the Biddulph service attributed to Swansea; the dish in

Figure 63. Swansea plates from the Biddulph service

Figure 64. A Coalport plate from the Biddulph service

figure 64 is described as of Coalport manufacture (pictures courtesy of Sotheby's, though the poorer quality of their reproduction is attributable to me, for which I apologize).

CHAPTER 13

Characteristics of the 'Weston Service'

The main features of this predominantly English service are that the teapot is French; the pieces have an individual design (with the exception of the teapot stand, which is the same as one of the saucers) and they have strong variations in translucency (both between and within individual pieces), dimensions and weight. This is illustrated, aside figures 66 – 89, but please note that the measurements are approximate and the translucency is on a subjective scale of 1–10. Therefore, the numbers are comparative not absolute. They are summarized below:

Variations in the saucers;
(i)   weight 95gm to 150gm
(ii)   diameter 132mm to 137mm
(iii)   height 26mm to 30mm
(iv)   translucency 6 to 9
Variations in the cups;
(i)   weight 100gm to125gm
(ii)   diameter 77mm to 82mm
(iii)   height 58mm to 62mm
(iv)   translucency 6 to 8
Variations in the cans;
(i)   weight 100gm to 125gm

Figure 65. De la Courtille teapot from the Weston service

(ii)   diameter 66mm to 68mm

iii)   height 60mm to 65mm

(iv)   translucency 5 to 7

On all items the painting is highlighted with gilt, to simulate bronzes of the classical period, though on some, the highlighting is almost rubbed off.

Six of the pieces within the service do not have individual gilt objects. These six pieces are the teapot (*fig. 65*) the jug (figures 5 & 6, chapter 2), one saucer (fig 74) and three cups (figures 71, 73 and 77); these cups each have a narrower band of gold round the rim than that found on the other cups. All six pieces are of particularly good translucency and all but the saucer include horses, or other animals, in their decoration. Similar animal forms are not found on the other pieces. These six then, could be said to form a sub-group within the service.

As the label on the teapot numbers 7 pieces of china, one possibility (there are others) is that it refers to these pieces, plus one other.

Figures 66–89 show English pieces from the Weston service.

Figure 66. Saucer, very good translucency (9);
wt 135 gm; diameter 115 mm; ht 30 mm.

Figure 67. Teapot stand, translucency poor and uneven, opaque in parts, best
areas 4. Wt 300 gm; ht 20 mm; oval dimensions
190 x 160 mm.

Figure 68. Saucer, quite poor translucency (6); wt 150 gm; diameter 136 mm, ht 30 mm. There is a slight yellowing on the inner rim. Possibly an incised mark near centre.

Figure 69. Saucer, quite good translucency (7); wt 140 gm; diameter 136 mm, ht 27 mm. Again there is slight yellowing on the inner rim. A potting circle, centre of underside.

Figure 70. Can, uneven translucency, best on the base, overall 6; wt 125 gm; ht 64 mm, diameter 67 mm.

Figure 71. Cup, very good translucency (8), better on the sides than base; wt 100 gm; ht 60 mm, diameter 77 mm.

Figure 72. Cup, quite poor translucency (6); wt 125 gm; ht 62 mm, diameter 79 mm. Hairline crack, virtually top to base.

Figure 73. Cup, very good translucency (8) on sides, base poor; wt 100 gm; ht 62 mm; diameter 82 mm. Repaired.

Figure 74. Saucer, very good translucency (9); wt 95 gm; diameter 135 mm; ht 26 mm. Potting circle, centre of underside.

Figure 75. Saucer, quite good translucency but uneven (7); wt 125 gm; diameter 133 mm; ht 27 mm. Possibly an incised mark near centre.

Figure 76. Cup, base opaque, sides quite good translucency (6);
wt 110 gm; ht 61 mm; diameter 80 mm.

Figure 77. Cup, very good translucency on sides (8), base poor;
wt 100 gm; ht 60 mm; diameter 81 mm.

Figure 78. Can, quite poor translucency (5), base the most translucent;
wt 130 gm; ht 65 mm; diameter 67 mm.

Figure 79. Can, quite good translucency (7), slightly uneven;
wt 100 gm; ht 64 mm; diameter 67 mm.

Figure 80. Can, quite good translucency (7), base best;
wt 110 gm; ht 60 mm; diameter 66 mm.

Figure 81. Saucer, quite poor, uneven translucency (6); wt 130 gm;
diameter 133 mm; ht 29 mm. Large potting circle, approx 1 cm inside outer rim.

Figure 82. Saucer, very good translucency (8); wt 110 gm;
diameter 137 mm; ht 28 mm.

Figure 83. Cup, quite poor translucency, uneven (6);
wt 100 gm; ht 58 mm; diameter 77 mm.

Figure 84. Cup, quite good translucency (7), sides better than base;
wt 100 gm; ht 60 mm; diameter 79 mm.

Figure 85. Can, quite poor translucency (5), base best;
wt 100 gm; ht 60 mm; diameter 68 mm. Small star crack on base.

Figure 86. Can, quite poor translucency (5); wt 110 gm; ht 60 mm; diameter 66 mm.

Figure 87. Saucer, quite good translucency (7), uneven; wt 115 gm; diameter 133 mm; ht 30 mm.

Figure 88. Cup, quite poor translucency (6); wt 110 gm; ht 60 mm; diameter 78 mm.

Figure 89. Saucer, quite good translucency (7), slightly uneven; wt 135 gm; diameter 135 mm; ht 30 mm. A potting circle, centre of underside.

It has already been said that there is a variation of translucency within the pieces as well as between them; it is noted also that the higher translucency areas are generally found within the walls of cups but bases of the cans.

The jug has a blue, smudged dot on the base (see figure 113, Appendix 1). To my untrained eye, the decoration, paler on the jug, is not as well executed as on some of the other pieces; though it may be something to do with the difficulties of painting on a piece of that shape.

To continue on the subject of decoration, it is interesting to note the more unusual, slightly macabre element introduced on, for example, figure 86, which depicts a lady demurely holding a head in, or made into something resembling a bag. Another point of interest is the similarities in the decoration on the two pieces, both saucers, that appear to have had incised marks; each feature one or more women with a musical instrument.

Neo-Classical style of decoration is not unique to this service, though not always as finely executed as on most of these pieces. Other examples have been found on both French and English porcelain and pottery. The English examples include Ridgway attributed wares and, perhaps more often, on 'outside decorated' pieces attributed to Coalport: one such piece is the French style cylindrical teapot, dated circa 1810, which can be found, as image 62, on the Ironbridge Gorge Museum's permanent internet gallery of 'Early Coalport Teawares'. The museum says of image 62:

> "*A number of Coalport shapes were decorated with Neo-Classical figures in a silhouette style by Thomas Baxter in London around this time. Baxter catered for a smart clientele suggesting this unusual teapot supplied an exclusive and fashionable taste.*"

Thomas Baxter was included in chapter 8, on artists.

In the meantime, there is another teapot that may be included here; it is not part of the 'Weston service' but is decorated in the same style. The owner of the teapot, in *figure 90*, is Brian Adams, keeper of the

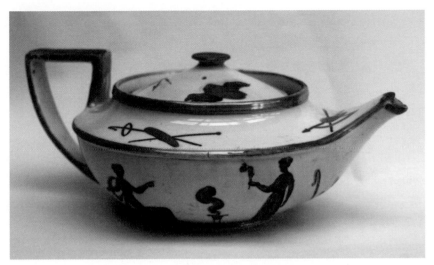

Figure 90. A teapot not from the Weston service but decorated in the same style

Bovey Tracey Heritage Museum, Devon. He has kindly given permission to publish the contents of a note, which was with the teapot when purchased from a "junk shop" some thirty years ago (which would make the purchase around 1978):

> *I guarantee that the/this teapot was the property of Sir Walter Scott while residing at Abbotsford and that it was given by a housekeeper there to the ? – - of Mr. Stewart, late Presbyterian minister at Stockton-on-Tees.*
>
>

J/T W Mac? — -
Vicar of St. John's Stockton-on-Tees. March 4th 1881/7

The prow style spout makes this teapot of a broader interest, the context of which belongs in Appendix 1.

At this stage there is nothing more that can be said about the characteristics of the service. Perhaps in years to come, if, for example, investigation of the chemical composition of various pieces becomes feasible, more will be learned and deduced. The service remains in private hands: accessibility through display in a museum could also help further our knowledge.

Further information

A return to the Jarvis papers, Lincolnshire archives, referred to previously – chapters 1; 6; 10: the great niece of George Ralph Payne Jarvis (G.R.P. Jarvis) was Henrietta Scott. Her personal papers, within the Jarvis papers, refer to a Rev. Alexander Scott who wrote to his Daughter Maria in 1838 from Southampton.

CHAPTER 14

Are We There Yet?*

The purpose of this book has been to explore the provenance that accompanied the 'Weston service' and determine the identity and thus connections, of the Mr Weston who commissioned the service and to determine also, if possible, from whom the commission was made.

To answer the question of this chapter simply, I would say 'yes'; the service was commissioned by Mr William Weston, an initial description of whom is given in chapter 4, from the potter Mr William Billingsley, whose career is outlined in chapter 1.

In chapter 2, several reasons were given that suggested Billingsley as a contender for the potter (I must emphasize that, here, I refer only to the commission). From subsequent research, strong additional support for Billingsley's involvement comes, firstly, from the fact that William Weston was in Gainsborough, close proximity to Billingsley's place of work, circa the period to which the service dates. There is a further strengthening from the several ways in which William Weston is found to connect with people whose lives relate to the work of William Billingsley; artists and other 'Westons' including Billingsley's patrons William Weston Young and Lewis Weston Dillwyn.

But perhaps it is too simple to answer 'yes'. Perhaps a similar argument could be made in favour of another potter. That does have to be a consideration and it has been.

Acknowledgments to Tess and Jack for the title of this chapter

Along the way, the Davenport factory was of interest. It seems possible that the Davenport potters may also connect with the Knight/Austen family (though if so, it seems more distantly than the Westons): that is, more or less, the extent of the case for Davenport.

A connection between the Rose family of Gainsborough (English, 1976) and the Roses of Coalport was speculated but no evidence was found to support such a notion.

Names have occurred that raise the possibility of relationships to other potters, for example Rathbone, Newbold, Barr and Yates. The exploration of these, especially perhaps Rose and Barr, may prove to be of further interest in another context, period and location but their short strands in the web of this particular story are weak. Conversely, the complicated Billingsley/Weston connections, and the Weston/Weston connections, strengthen the more the web is untangled. There is surely more to come.

As was pointed out in chapter one, many factories experimented with ceramic bodies but I know of none, other than William Billingsley, that was so persistent in pursuing an aim such as his, to match the combined qualities of early soft paste French porcelain and the early hard paste German porcelains. Nor were other factories as likely to include French pieces as part of a service commissioned from their own factory: the provenance suggests the marked French teapot was not a replacement piece.

Taking all into account, I feel confident to assert that it was William Billingsley who was to make Mr Weston his service. We are 'there', but where do we go next?

To conclude, from that assertion, that all the English pieces currently part of this service were produced at Brampton–in–Torksey is a leap I am not prepared to take.

The peculiar history of Billingsley at Brampton, requires that porcelain pieces have, ideally, provenance, mark and an attributable form, before a positive attribution to that factory can be made; two of the three would probably suffice. We have the provenance.

Other than a few words in chapter 2, little has been said about the important work of Roy Chapman on the excavated shards from the Brampton site. Insightful articles by R. Chapman, (which are recommended for any readers interested in this aspect) can be found in several of the listed sources of information (Chapman 1995, Deverill et al 1999, Gray 2003, Usher Gallery 1996). What follows is but a small fraction of what has been described by Roy Chapman in those articles.

From around *"0.5 tonnes of porcelain wasters and small kiln furniture"*, markings were found on several hundred shards. These comprised an incised mark of any letter, or, of a number within the range of 1 to 13. There was also one waster, a base, that had an underglaze blue mark; that fragment had *"triple-pitting of the 3 cockspurs"*, that is three sets of three points, arranged as triangles, *fig 91*. Most of the pieces are in biscuit form and the incised marks may become invisible in normal light after glazing. The ceramic body

Figure 91. Triple-pitting of 3 cockspurs, Brampton base
(Photograph courtesy of R Chapman)

provides limited aid to identification: *"Amongst the biscuit ware, there is a wide range of bodies – from a very glassy body with an almost Swansea-like translucence, to shards that could more usefully be described as fine earthenware"*.

There are two pieces in the 'Weston service' which may possibly have incised marks, but these are not properly discernible, even with the aid of a powerful transmitted light. Both of these pieces are saucers, figs 68 & 75, but with quite different specifications.

The third thing to consider is the shape, an arduous task to reconstruct: *figure 92* shows just a small collection of Brampton shards; *figure 93* some of the progress Roy Chapman has made; *figure 94* a partially reconstructed Brampton cup.

Although shapes, unique, so far, to Brampton, have been expertly re-formed, many others match those that Billingsley produced at Pinxton, and some have a similarity to Coalport or to Minton.

The work of Roy Chapman has taken us a long way and it

Figure 92. Box of Brampton shards

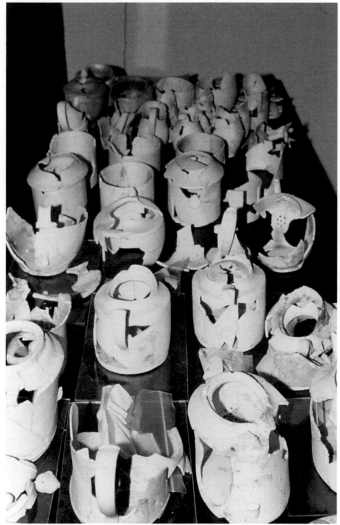

Figure 93. Largely reconstructed oval hollow-wares, Brampton
(Photograph courtesy of R Chapman)

continues to increase our knowledge substantially, but, as he acknowledges *"the material recovered from this very small area of the site is extremely unlikely to represent the full range of forms being produced at the factory over the whole of its short life"*. And, at least for the larger hollow-wares that have been reconstructed, *"almost all are represented in all types of body"*. So, again, they are exciting discoveries but the application is limited as regards making a positive attribution to Brampton.

Figure 94. Partially reconstructed Brampton cup

Figure 95. Handle on Pinxton cup compared with handle on Weston service
cup

It follows, therefore, that although the English forms within the 'Weston service' are not discounted, they are without any distinguishing characteristics that contribute to a positive attribution. The bute shape cups could be likened to Brampton or Pinxton cups in every respect other than the finer details of the handles; a difference not apparent from photographs alone, *figure 95*.

The well known phrase 'absence of evidence is not evidence of absence' is aptly applied in this instance.

Of note, is the oval stand in the 'Weston service'. Its pattern is the only one repeated in the service (compare figure 67 with the saucer, figure 81). Also, its presence suggests that, at some stage, there may have been another teapot, of an oval rather than round shape: in his first chapter on *European Porcelain*, Geoffrey Godden refers to the unusual inclusion of an oval (perhaps English) teapot and stand, alongside a French cylindrical pot in the 'de la Courtille' service decorated by William Billingsley at Brampton.

Dr Godden, in the same chapter, notes the difficulties faced, on occasion, to distinguish between French porcelain decorated in its factory of origin and that imported in the white, then decorated in England after the French fashion. This is returned to in appendix 1 as part of a general discussion.

The main ceramic interest in the body of this book is the 'Weston service' and in this respect the sub-group of pieces, referred to in the previous chapter, is of particular interest: The teapot and probably the jug are of French manufacture but the others are English. I would deem the pieces of this sub-group, with the possible exception of the saucer, to have been decorated by the same hand and, therefore, decorated in England.

Perhaps the English pieces of this sub-group were made and decorated at Brampton; perhaps not. Perhaps some of the other pieces were matched and decorated at an outside decorating establishment; perhaps not. Perhaps Thomas Baxter's studio was one such establishment involved with the service; perhaps not.

Much, regarding production and decoration, comes down to personal opinion and interpretation of circumstances. Other enthusiasts of ceramics, with far more experience than I have, have failed to reach a consensus; some have seen only photographs, some a single piece, others the whole service (*figure 96* shows a group examining the service, from left to right, as viewed, Michael Bailey, Roy Chapman and Ewan Semper). Importantly, all opinions were given before the start of this book and, therefore, without full knowledge of the findings of the research into the provenance.

This part has been relatively straightforward; the documents found and facts therein are indisputable. Attribution of manufacture and decoration will always be open to debate. Should a consensus be

Figure 96. Left to right, as viewed, Michael Bailey, Roy Chapman, Ewan Semper

reached at any point, it is liable, over time, to be challenged. That is the nature of research and is how it should be; that is what keeps the interest in antique ceramics alive.

APPENDIX

Extrapolation of the X Factor

The question of attribution of ceramics of the late 18[th]century and
early 19th century is often a tricky one. Much has been written in
other publications on such considerations as factory records; the type of
ceramic body; shape; pattern and comparisons with any marked pieces.

The paucity of known Brampton- in-Torksey pieces and the
peculiar background of that factory increase the usual difficulties and
make the existence of any provenance an additional, significant
consideration.

Apart from the plates, *figure 97*, which were known to have come
from Creake Abbey, none of the pots illustrated in this appendix has
any known provenance. Mostly, they have a place in this discussion
because they do not quite 'fit'. I would describe them as having
something unusual about them, except that there are so many such
misfits around that it renders such a description inaccurate.

The gilt and floral decoration on the lobed earthenware plates, *fig. 97*, is
of an unusually high standard for earthenware, of a type expected to be
found on a porcelain body. *Figure 98* shows the triple spur points, the
same arrangement on the bases of both plates; there are three sets of three
points around the rim and one widely spaced set of three in the centre.

Both of the simply but well painted dessert dishes in *figure 99* could

Figure 97. A pair of Earthenware plates

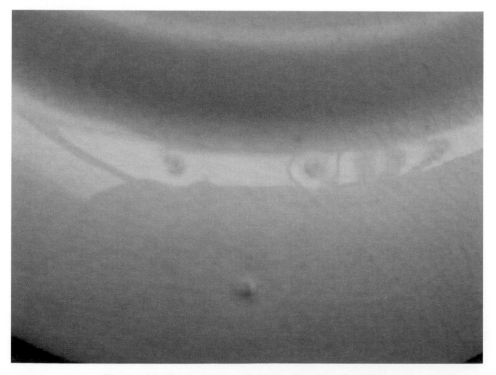

Figure 98. Triple spur points on the rim of a plate

easily fit within the same service, though they were not found together. Only one has any markings; the one with the rose has an incised X. As far as I am aware, few English factories (with the possible exception of Brampton) regularly used incised marks: A 'scratched X' is to be found on some very early Worcester; a scratched, or incised B is found on some Barr Worcester, a scratched G on Grainger Worcester; pieces with an incised 7 have sometimes been attributed to Coalport (not always with absolute confidence).

Another piece in this group to have an incised X, occurs on the teapot of prow shape, *figure 100*. As yet, I have not come across an identical pattern elsewhere. A pattern with some similarity is Pinxton pattern number 275.

The prow shape is an interesting one. I refer back to *figure 90*, chapter 13; of prow shape in that it has a spout seamless with the body but has a round, rather than oval, base. This, I believe to be an unusual shape, although another example can be found (plate 1760, Miller & Berthoud, 1985), decorated in neo-classical motifs (no figures) in sepia and gilt. That example was attributed to Coalport but - as it is not of a usual Coalport shape and possibly outside decorated - it is not clear on what basis.

A *Directory of British Teapots* (Berthoud & Maskell, 2006), informative section (11) on the oval prow, features a dozen teapots and throws up another interesting variant difficult to attribute (plate 857). The description reads *"Unidentified, c 1805, hybrid hard paste porcelain, variant shape with a double ring finial, loop handle rising from the shoulder rather than the collar, the pattern number, a cursive 'P' and '131' suggesting Pinxton (although Pinxton 131 is different*), possibly decorated by Billingsley at Torksey. Ht 6in (152mm)"*.

* I own to being somewhat confused by this comment: the pattern on the illustrated teapot appears to match that described under Pinxton pattern 131: *"Double handle cup and saucer marked P.131 in gilding. **A border of cabbage roses on a burnished ground.** M. Steele Sale, 26th June, 1962 ...Sotheby's ..."* (cited in Sheppard, 1996).

Figure 99. Two dessert dishes, one with incised X

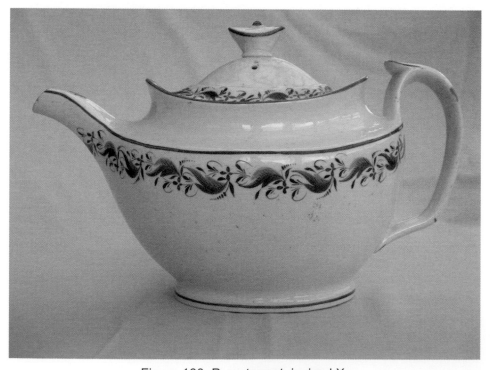

Figure 100. Prow teapot, incised X

One pattern that was common to several factories is variously referred to as the 'blue harebell' or the 'bluebell'. There are known examples marked with an impressesd FBB (Flight, Barr and Barr, Worcester: other examples of this pattern include a Derby (puce) marked, 24 fluted tea bowl, with a gilt inside border pictured (Berthoud 1990, plate 87) aside (Berthoud 1990, plate 88) an unidentified, 32 fluted tea bowl. The latter example has a 'scratched G' mark and is described as 'of beautiful white translucency'.

The tea bowl in *figure 101* is similar to the unidentified bowl in plate 88, in that it also has 32 flutes and is of a beautiful white translucency. However, this bowl has 32 harebells – one on each facet – whereas the Berthoud example has 16 harebells – one to every two facets; the dimensions differ and it has an incised S on its base instead of a G.

An example of a piece with an incised X and in the blue harebell

Figure 101. Harebell patterned teabowl, incised S

pattern is the cup in *figure 102*. The gilt inside border on this cup corresponds to that on the Berthoud, plate 87, Derby bowl, referred to above; the cup shape and handle can be compared to a characteristic shape of Flight/ Barr Worcester.

The number of New Hall's harebell pattern has not been identified but the pattern has been noted (u256, Preller, 2003).

The Greek key pattern was used almost universally and the addition of oak leaves was made by several factories. The can in *figure 103* is the popular pattern in gilt. Sheppard, 1996, illustrates a cup and saucer in this pattern, sold as one lot, of Pinxton manufacture; the cup was Pinxton but the saucer was Spode, marked.

A Pinxton variation of the pattern has green leaves in place of gilt. Under pattern number 347 Sheppard says *"Breakfast cup and saucer, with a gilt Grecian Key pattern band set between two gold lines, from which are suspended green oak leaves. A most unusual type of decoration, marked P. No.*

Figure 102. Harebell patterned cup, incised X

Figure 103. Greek key and oak leaf pattern, gilt

347" He goes on to say that there is some confusion as a Pinxton can with a different pattern had also been given the number 347 (cites J. Meeks, 1992, *A Beginners Guide to Pinxton China*). *Figure 104* is one of two similar cans found in this 'Pinxton' pattern. The handles on these cans do not sit comfortably; they have a creamy glaze and are thickly potted whereas the cans are brilliant white, thinly potted and highly translucent.

The cup and saucer in *figure 105* are both of Spode pattern 742, introduced 1805, they came together but appear to be a match: the cup, marked with a blue under glaze M, is of a greater translucency and the faint crazing of the glaze is absent on the saucer.

Figure 106 is a handled can, not of a Derby shape but bears a Derby styled factory mark on the base. The unmarked can, *figure 107*, was

Figure 104. Greek key with green oak leaves pattern

Figure 105. Spode's pattern 742

Figure 106. Can bearing a Derby styled mark

Figure 107. Rose and trellis design

described, in a catalogued auction, as from the Derby factory but, again, is not of a Derby shape. This error was presumably made because of the rose and trellis design, well known on Derby pieces; it has also been found on Mason and Coalport pieces.

Another version of the rose and trellis design can be seen on the unmarked cup and saucer of *figure 108*. The grooved, square handled, bucket shaped cup is similar to one produced at Derby.

Any Derby type piece that is unmarked has to be treated with caution; it may be Derby but more likely is not.

Figure *109* shows the handle and part of a well marked, positively attributed Derby cup, overlapping an unrelated and unmarked (save a small number 21 written in black) Derby type saucer. The previous caution must apply but this unmarked piece is more convincing as Derby than the other foregoing examples: its feel, colour, crazing and slight staining, match well the positively attributed Derby. A case when the handling of the pieces is of utmost importance.

In chapter 14, Dr Godden's comments regarding the difficulties

Figure 108. A square handled cup in a rose trellis pattern

Figure 109. Similarities of a marked Derby piece with an unmarked piece

that can arise in locating the country of decoration on French porcelain (Godden, 1993) were cited. I now return to those difficulties.

The Angouleme cornflower pattern, featured on the can in *figure 110*, is so called because the pattern was popularized by the factory of that name (the factory at times known as Guerhard & Dihl or simply Dihl). The can is unmarked but in this case the porcelain is probably English.

A delightful pattern, to my mind, is the addition of poppies to an Angouleme type border. The example in *figure 111* is on a French porcelain teapot, bearing the mark of the Comte d'Artois factory. A similarly styled pattern is on the plate in *figure 112*. This is included as a point of interest as it has a blue dot on the base which matches, in size and colour, the blue dot on the base of the Weston jug (*fig 113*; the jug is closer to the camera and, therefore, the dot appears larger in comparison). But this popular French pattern was also popular in English factories. For example Minton, in their first period of producing

Figure 110. Angouleme cornflower pattern

Figure 111. A French teapot in the poppy pattern

Figure 112. A plate in the poppy pattern

Figure 113. Dot on base of plate is compared to that on base of
'Weston' jug

porcelain, had a version of the poppy design, pattern number 70; Pinxton's pattern 104 had a band of similarly bold poppies, but differed in other respects.

Before we leave poppies, the English can and saucer, *figure 114*, is quite intriguing. The decoration appears to have been clobbered; the poppies cleverly applied over the top of a continuous cornflower border. The blue glaze is an unusual addition. In spite of the full decoration, the high translucency of the saucer remains apparent.

It is the blue ground of the preceding can and saucer that prompts the inclusion of the slightly warped plate, *figure 115*. It is a curious mix of quality and poor taste. The porcelain appeals and is highly translucent; as with the previous piece, the translucency is in spite of full decoration. Therein lies the poor taste. The decoration does nothing to enhance the plate; the blue ground is uneven and the moulded border is lost beneath it.

Figure 114. A poppy pattern probably clobbered

Figure 115. Translucent plate with a blue ground

The full decoration on the next item, the cache-pot in *figure 116*, also could be said to be detracting from the white, high translucency of the porcelain. The ground colour is an unusual, dull, greenish turquoise, which has run in places, see *figure 117*. However, I find the overall effect of the decoration pleasing. (This piece has incised markings.)

It is not the purpose of this appendix to attempt attribution of the pieces featured so far. Quite the contrary.

There are several known circumstances of production that can account for apparent misfits; plagiarism of both patterns and shapes; replacement pieces produced by a factory other than that of the original

Figure 116. Turquoise ground cache pot

Figure 117. Uneven ground colour

Figure 118. A Pinxton cup

– in which case, a factory mark may sometimes also be copied. And there are likely many other simple explanations to be found.

The purpose of this appendix is to give a place to pieces sometimes shunned by collectors because of the very thing that makes them interesting – their relative anonymity.

These such finds, if they can be brought together in sufficient numbers, and studied alongside more conventional collections, are what will help to move on our level of knowledge.

I conclude with a cup, *figure 118*, that would now fit nicely into a conventional Pinxton collection: the pattern is featured (Sheppard, 1996) on a teapot of known Pinxton shape; the cup has an impressed capital G, 1/8" high (a typical way of marking Pinxton); and the angular handle on the cup is accepted (when other factors concur) as Pinxton. Interestingly, Barry Sheppard notes, in respect of another

Pinxton angular handled cup, *"cup and saucer which in the 1968 era when the shards came to light would not have been accepted as Pinxton by the majority of collectors because of the angular handle"*. A lesson we need to remember.

Sources of Information

A$_2$A – *Access to Archives*: an on-line resource provided by National Archives, which gives catalogue listings and abstracts of documents held in district archive and record offices. Too numerous to individually list all those used; a selection is given below:

Bristol Record Office: *Haynes Collection*
Centre for Buckinghamshire Studies: *Lee Family of Hartwell*
    Lovett family of Liscombe Park
Cheshire & Chester Archives: *Brooke of Norton Collection*
    Cholmondeley of Cholmondeley
Derbyshire Record Office: *Chandos Pole family of Radbourne*
    Wilmot-Horton of Osmaston & Catton
Devon Record Office: *Dayman of Ashley Court, Tiverton*
Guildhall Library: *Records of Sun Fire Office*
Hampshire Record Office: *Knollis family, Earls of Banbury*
Hertfordshire Archives: *Pryor family of Weston Park*
Lincolnshire Archives: *Jarvis*
London Metropolitan Archives: *Angerstein family*
    Chandos family papers
Nottinghamshire Archives: *Bulwell estates*
    Lothian of Melbourne
Oxfordshire Record Office: *Bradwell Grove Estate*
Plymouth & West Devon Record Office: *Morley of Saltram*
Shakespeare Birthplace Trust Records Office: *Leigh of Stoneleigh*
Surrey History Centre: *Somers Cocks family of Reigate Priory*

172   BILLINGSLEY, THE WESTON CONNECTION...

Warwickshire County Record Office: *Canal Records*
Wolverhampton Archives: *Title deeds to the Oxley Estate*

Bailey M. Personal communication, gratefully received 2006.

Bailey M. *The Northern Ceramic Society, Newsletter no. 151, September 2008*

Baxter T. *Egyptian, Grecian, and Roman Costume* Pub. William Miller, Albermarle Street, 1810.

Berthoud M. *A Compendium of British Cups* Pub. Micawber, 1990

Berthoud M. & Maskell R. *A Directory of British Teapots* Pub. Micawber, 2006

Burke J *A General and Heraldic Dictionary of the Peerage and Baronetage of The British Empire* 4th Edition, Vols 1 & 11, Pub. Colburn and Bentley, London, 1832

Chapman R.E. *'Excavation of the Torksey Porcelain Manufactory' English Ceramic Circle Transactions,* Vol 15, Part 3, 1995, (from a paper read at the Linnean Society Rooms, Dec 1993).

Deverill I. & Sheppard A.B. editors and contributors *Billingsley, Mansfield, Bicentenary* Pub. Pinxton Society, 1999

Dorment R *British Painting in the Philadelphia Museum of Art* Pub. Philadelphia Museum of Art, 1986

English J.S. *Gainsborough: Some links with America* Pub. Friends of the Old Hall Association, Gainsborough, by permission of The Lincolnshire Arts Supporters' Society, 1976

Exley C.L. *A History of the Torksey and Mansfield China Factories* Pub. G.R.G. Exley,1970

Fitzimons N. *Benchmarks in Civil Engineering* original article 1967, from Finch J.K. & Fitzimons N, editor and contributor *Engineering Classics ... Selected papers from The Consulting Engineer,* Pub. Cedar Press, 1978

Glover S. (compiler) Noble T. (editor) *The History of the county of Derby* Pub. Glover, printed by Mozley & Son, Derby, 1829

Godden G. A. *Oriental Export Market Porcelain* Pub. Granada, 1979

Godden G. A. *Coalport & Coalbrookdale Porcelains* Pub. Antiques

Collectors' Club, 1981

Godden G. A. Editor and Main Author *Staffordshire Porcelain* Pub. Granada, 1983

Godden G.A. *Godden's Guide to European Porcelain* Pub. Barrie & Jenkins, 1993

Godden G.A. Personal communication, gratefully received, 2008

Gray J. editor and contributor *Welsh Ceramics in Context* Pub. Royal Institution of South Wales, Part I 2003, Part II 2005.

Haslem J. *The Old Derby China Factory: The Workmen and Their Productions.* Pub. George Bell & sons, London, 1876

Herbert-Young N. Personal communication, gratefully received, 2006

Ingilby Sir Thomas. Personal communication, gratefully received, 2007

Institution of Civil Engineers, One George Street, Westminster, London, SW1P 3AA. The assistance given by the staff is greatly appreciated.

Jacks L. *The Great Houses of Nottinghamshire and the County Families* Pub. W & A.S. Bradshaw, Nottingham, 1881

John W.D. *Swansea Porcelain* Pub. Ceramic Book Company, Newport, 1958

John W.D. *William Billingsley (1758 – 1828)* Pub. Lonsdale & Bartholomew (Bath) Ltd., 1968

Knowles J. *The Life and Writings of Henry Fuseli* Pub. Henry Colburn, Richard Bentley, London, 1831

Leeds University Library, Special Collections, Woodhouse Lane, Leeds LS2 9JT. The assistance given by the staff is greatly appreciated.

Le Faye Deirdre *Jane Austen, A family Record* Pub. Cambridge University Press, 2004

Le Faye Deirdre editor *Jane Austen's Letters* Pub. Oxford University Press, 2003

Lenton Local History Society, *Lenton Times* lentontimes.co.uk (www.)

Lincolnshire Archives, St. Rumbold Street, Lincoln LN2 5AB

Maddison A.R. editor *Lincolnshire Pedigrees V2* London,1903

Manchip D Personal communication, gratefully received, 2006

Mansfield Museum, Leeming Street, Mansfied, Nottinghamshire
NG18 1NG. The assistance given by the staff is greatly
appreciated.

Messenger M. *Coalport 1795 -1926* Pub. Antique Collectors' Club, 1995

Miller P & Berthoud M *Anthology of British Teapots* Pub. Micawber,
1985

Morris R Personal communication, gratefully received, 2006

National Archives, Kew, London: Chancery documents and wills, too
numerous to list individually but some key ones identified in
the text.

National Maritime Museum, Greenwich, London

Neath Antiquarian Society, West Glamorgan Archive Service,
Swansea

Owen J.V., Wilstead J.O., Williams R.W., Day T.E. *'A Tale of Two Cities:
Compositional Characteristics of some Nantgarw and Swansea
Porcelains and their Implications for Kiln Wastage' Journal of
Archaeological Science*, Vol. 25, Issue 4, April 1998, pp 359-375

Preller P *A partial reconstruction of the NEW HALL PATTERN BOOK*
Pub. Pat Preller, Bude, 2003

Robinson A. *The Last Man Who Knew Everything* Pearson Education,
Inc., 2005

Shead, jim-shead.com (www.) An informative website on the subject
of canals

Sheppard C.B. *PinxtonPorcelain 1795 – 1813*, Pub. C. Barry Sheppard,
1996

Skempton, A.W. et al., editors *Biographical Dictionary of Civil
Engineers, Vol. 1* Pub. Thomas Telford on behalf of the Institution
of Civil Engineers, 2002

Smiles S. *Lives of the Engineers, Smeaton and Rennie* Pub. John Murray,
London, 1904

Staveley P. Personal communication, gratefully received, 2006.
Further information now available on c.d. *The Staveley Clan:
1,000 Years of Staveley Family History,* proceeds of sales go to the

charity 'Future Hope'

stirnet.com (www.) A well researched and referenced site of genealogy. Membership and fee are required. I used it sparingly but leads were borne out from other sources as correct.

Usher Gallery *Not just a bed of Roses* Pub. Usher Gallery, Lincoln et al, 1996. The assistance given by the staff is greatly appreciated.

Wilstead. J.O & Morris B. *Thomas Baxter The Swansea Years 1816 1819* Pub. Gibbs Charitable Trust and Glynn Vivian Art Gallery. 1997.

wrexham.gov.uk (www.)